Air Fryer Cookbook UK

The Ultimate Air Fryer Recipe Book Guide with Over 100 Easy, Simple & Delicious UK Recipes. Pro Tips & Recipe Index Included.

Olivia Taylor

Hey there!

I would like to thank you for your trust, and I really hope you'll enjoy the book.

A lot of thought and effort went into creating the book. I am not a part of a big publishing company and I take care of the whole publishing process myself in an effort to make sure your cooking journey is as smooth as possible.

If for any reason you did not like the book you can write on my email at deliciousrecipes.publishing@gmail.com. I always make sure to get back to everybody and if you're not happy with the book I can share another book.

I'm trying really hard to create the best cookbooks I can and I'm always open to constructive criticism.

Enjoy!

Fundamentals of Air Fryer Cooking

When it comes to air frying, there are a few things that you need to know before you get started. Firstly, air frying is not exactly like deep frying foods. An air fryer mostly depends on air, not fat, to convey heat to the food, and that makes for a different result. Do not cook expecting a like-for-like but healthier alternative to your favourite fried snack; you won't be pleased with the outcome!

However, air fryers are still excellent tools if you use them properly, and they can massively reduce the number of calories in your food while still allowing you to enjoy a super crispy, crunchy meal. Food cooked in an air fryer has many advantages, so let's cover a few of those. The first is that air frying is a cheap way to get delicious food, because you will use vastly less oil than in traditional frying, which can get through oil fast. High-quality oils tend to be expensive, so air frying is a great way to reduce your food budget without cutting back on the quality. Next, air frying is a great way to make vegetables taste amazing. Forget boiled broccoli and steamed sprouts; an air fryer can really hype up vegetables and make them crispy and delicious. They are a fantastic option with few additional calories because they have mostly been cooked in hot air, and this is a wonderful way to make your diet healthier.

Coupled with that, even if you're not opting for vegetables, air frying is a healthier choice than deep frying. You might not be getting all the nutrients found in fried veggies, but you can rest assured that at least your chicken isn't also dripping in grease. This helps if you struggle to enjoy vegetables, but you still want to make your diet better overall. Furthermore, air fryers are very quick, which is great if you have a busy life – and who doesn't? When you're struggling to get dinner on the table in time, an air fryer is a good way to reduce cooking times and spend fewer hours in the kitchen.

Finally, air frying is considerably safer than traditional deep frying. You don't have a huge pan full of scalding oil, with the potential for spitting and spills. While you may be a pro at frying safely, it's still better to avoid this entirely, and an air fryer lets you cook without the burning hot pan. Overall, there are a lot of reasons to air fry your foods, so let's find out how you can get a great start to your air frying journey by exploring some of the common mistakes and how to avoid them.

Common Air Frying Mistakes You Must Avoid

You'll find your air fryer is a much more useful piece of equipment if you use it carefully and don't make some of these common mistakes. Cooking without knowing how to operate your air fryer can spoil the taste or texture of your food, and may make the process much more frustrating. So, what mistakes should you avoid making with your fryer?

Failing to Dry Foods

Your air fryer will work much better if you use it on foods that are dry on the outside. If you put in foods that are very wet, they will steam, rather than frying. The result, while it may be nice, will not be nearly as good as the crispy, fried version you can achieve by putting in reasonably dry foods.

Solve this problem by patting foods on a clean towel or piece of kitchen towel before you put them into your air fryer. You should do this with any vegetables that are wet on the outsides, as well as any meats. This extra step should take just a few seconds, and will result in superior fried food.

Failing to Preheat the Fryer

Like many cooking appliances, an air fryer needs to be heated in order to cook the food properly. If you are following a recipe, it might tell you how hot the fryer needs to be before you put the food in.

Don't be tempted to skip this step. An unheated air fryer will produce undercooked or soggy food, and that defeats the whole purpose of using the air fryer. You might also find that food doesn't cook evenly, because some parts of the fryer will be hotter than others when you add the food.

Instead, make sure you heat the air fryer to temperature before you put the food in. On the whole, three minutes should be enough for an air fryer to heat sufficiently. Putting food in a cold fryer will probably result in longer cook times, so you don't really save yourself any time by skipping the preheating step.

Overfilling the Air Fryer

Your food needs a good amount of airflow in order to cook properly in the air fryer, so make sure you aren't overfilling the basket.

If you add a whole lot of food all at once, you'll likely find that the food on the outside cooks well, but the food on the inside stays raw or goes soggy, because it is heating up without getting crispy.

Since the whole point of an air fryer is to provide lovely, crispy foods, you need to maximise the food's contact with the hot air. Instead of cramming your air fryer full, try to cook in small portions. This might take a little longer, but it will get the best possible results.

Using the Wrong Amount of Oil

Pay attention to how much oil your recipe calls for, and don't ignore this. Some recipes won't require any oil at all, but most will want a little bit to help aid that crispiness and add a bit of flavour. If the recipe calls for oil, don't omit it.

The fryer should be able to make deliciously crispy food without a lot of oil, but don't be afraid to use a bit. Brush foods lightly or buy a spray-on oil to ensure a thin and even coating.

Equally, don't add too much. Remember, air fryers aren't designed to cook with a lot of oil in them and foods should definitely not be dripping when you add them to the fryer. Oil dripping through the tray in the fryer can cause smoke, which will ruin your food and make your kitchen smell horrible.

Failing to Clean Your Fryer

Don't assume that because your air fryer depends upon air for its cooking, you don't need to clean it. You do; failing to keep your fryer clean will result in burnt, unpleasant smells and tastes that may transfer to your next meal.

Almost everything you put in an air fryer will leave at least some residue, so clean it after each use, even if it doesn't look too bad. You can't usually put the air fryer parts in your dishwasher, but a quick wash with some mild soapy water is generally all it needs to keep it clean.

It's best to do this as soon as the fryer has cooled down a bit; this avoids foods getting caked on and ensures you will remember to do it. Make this a habit any time you use the air fryer, and you'll keep it fresh and ready for your next cooking session.

How Air Frying Helps with Weight Loss

Many people purchase an air fryer because they know it will help them lose weight, so let's explore how that works.

The main reason that an air fryer will help you lose weight is that it reduces the amount of fat on the foods you consume. You do not need much (if any) oil to cook foods in an air fryer, so you can massively reduce your intake of fats. For example, where a deep-fried dish might require you to fry foods in about three-quarters of a litre of oil (although you won't consume all of this), an air-fried alternative would probably only need about 15 ml. It's easy to see how making this change could massively reduce the quantity of fat that you consume.

Air fried food is also generally lower in calories, which means that you can eat the same foods and be consuming far fewer calories overall. This can make weight management easier, especially if you eat a lot of fried foods.

Fried foods – unsurprisingly – are associated with poor diets and obesity, but for people who consume a lot of fried food, it can be very difficult to swap to radically different foods. Roasting and steaming are alternative cooking methods, but they don't produce a similar texture, and it can be very challenging to get used to them.

An air fryer represents a good middle ground, allowing the user to get the crispy foods that they enjoy with a much smaller quantity of fat involved. This can either be used as a way to transition to even better foods and cooking methods, or seen as an end goal in which oil consumption has at least been reduced.

How to Use Your Air Fryer for Weight Loss

We'll now explore some tips that will help you maximize the effectiveness of your air fryer for reducing your weight.

Reduce the Oil

Obviously, especially after the previous section, the biggest advantage that an air fryer has over a deep fat fryer is the decreased amount of fatty oil that you will consume. You will have to reduce the amount of oil you use to at least some degree, or you will end up with a smoky air fryer.

You may find that it helps to get a spray-on oil or use a brush to add a thin coating to your food's exterior. This will help you to decrease how much oil you use. Dipping your foods in oil will make them too greasy, and prevent you from getting the full benefit from using your fryer.

Remember, the less oil you can use (within reason), the better!

Alter Your Recipes

If you're serious about losing weight by using an air fryer, it's often a good idea to alter your recipes a bit. This will work in conjunction with the healthier cooking method, and the double-pronged approach is much more likely to give you good, quick results than simply eating the same foods, fried using hot air rather than oil.

As an example of this, if you swap to cooking chips in an air fryer but still eat them every night, you may not see a significant improvement to your weight, because you are still consuming a large amount of potato. While you have reduced or cut out the oil, you need to do a little more.

Reheating already fried foods in your air fryer is not the way to lose weight. Precooked foods like fries and fish sticks have probably already been deep-fried, and you won't make them a healthier option just because you air fry them for the second cook. It is much better to cook from scratch where you can.

Focus on Vegetables

Remember, air fryers are a great way to give yourself crispy vegetables to enjoy. If you find vegetables challenging, make the most of the new texture options and always include at least one vegetable group when you make a meal. Play around with the different vegetables and see how they fare in the air fryer. Find some favourites and make yourself incorporate them regularly.

Don't Use Your Air Fryer Every Day

An air fryer is a great alternative to deep frying foods, but there are other good cooking options, and the air fryer isn't the healthiest alternative there is. It works well to help you wean yourself away from fried foods and it is certainly a better option, but don't depend too heavily on it.

You should aim to use it in conjunction with other cooking choices, e.g. roasting, boiling, steaming, grilling. It shouldn't be your 'go to' for every day, or you probably won't find that you lose much weight! As part of your kitchen toolkit, it's a great addition, but it is not a cooking method to use exclusively.

Air Fryer FAQ

With all that in mind, let's look at a few ways in which you can get the best possible use out of your air fryer to ensure maximum enjoyment from everything you cook in it. Here are some common questions people have about their fryers.

How to Make Meals Extra Crispy

Since air fryers are perfect for creating crispy food, it's highly frustrating to cook in one and then find out that you don't get exactly that – crispy food. There are a few things you can do to ensure that your food comes out crunchy and delicious every time, however.

Firstly, make sure you aren't crowding the food too much. This results in steamed, soggy meals. Secondly, pat damp foods dry before adding them to the fryer. Again, this prevents steaming from occurring instead of frying.

Thirdly, preheat your air fryer so the food is hitting a hot basket and starting to sizzle immediately. Finally, don't forget to add a little bit of oil. While you want the air to do most of the work and crisping to keep the food healthy, just a dab of oil will help to lend your food a wonderful crunch factor.

How to Prevent Food From Sticking to the Air Fryer

Once again, the oil is important here. Although air fryers do come with a non-stick coating, if you don't grease your air fryer lightly before use, you may find that dinner has welded itself to the basket and you have to scrape it off, which may damage the coating. This is particularly true of older fryers, where the non-stick coating may have worn away.

Therefore, you need to add a thin layer of grease to the air fryer. Do not use a spray oil for this, as these can damage the coating further. Instead, dip a small brush in some oil and wipe it over the basket.

Make sure you are using oil with a high smoke point, such as sunflower oil, corn oil, or almond oil, because your air fryer is going to get very hot. Oils with a low smoke point, like extra virgin olive oil, should not be used because the temperatures are going to exceed what they can cope with.

How to Properly Clean an Air Fryer

We mentioned earlier that you need to clean your air fryer regularly, but make sure you don't put any parts of it in your dishwasher unless the manual says that this is okay. Obviously, the main appliance is electric and should never be submerged in water or put in the dishwasher.

After each use, you should remove the basket, pan, and tray and wash them in warm, soapy water. If food residue is stuck, leave them to soak for a bit and then gently scrub with a non-abrasive brush. Allow them to fully dry before putting them back in the fryer. You can also wipe the inside of the fryer down with a damp, slightly soapy cloth (let it cool first).

You should also check the heating coil for oil spills occasionally. If you find any, make sure that the unit is cool and then carefully wipe it with a damp cloth.

Cleaning your fryer regularly will help to avoid stubborn grease build ups and make it easier to cook in. Avoid using abrasive tools on your air fryer parts; these will ruin the non-stick coating, and may render the fryer useless.

Can I Just Swap My Normal Recipes Over?

You can use many normal recipes in your air fryer, but you do need to make some adjustments. The temperature and cooking time will likely need some alteration, and this is going to be a bit of trial-and-error, as every fryer is different and needs different allowances to be made.

As a rough guide, reduce the cooking temperature by a few degrees (around 5-10° C) and take about 20% off the cooking time. So, if your recipe says to cook for forty minutes at 150° C, try cooking for around thirty minutes at 145° C. Remember, you can always give the food a few more minutes if it isn't yet cooked, so it's better to have a lower time and temperature than to burn the food.

As long as you make allowances for time and temperature, many of your recipes can just be swapped without needing other significant changes.

Can I Open the Basket to Check on My Food?

Yes, you can open the basket to check on your food whenever you like, and simply slide it back in after. This is great when you're working out how long a recipe will take to cook; just check on the food every so often, and make a note of the overall cooking time so you'll know next time.

Do I Need to Shake the Basket?

You don't need to, but shaking the food around in the basket will help you achieve a crispy outer coating all over the food. It ensures any parts of the food that are touching other parts get moved and get their fair share of hot air crisping them.

Do this a couple of times during the cooking process, and you'll soon have delicious, crispy food to enjoy.

What Size Air Fryer Should I Buy?

Air fryers are surprisingly large for the amount of cooking capacity they offer, which is one of their slight disadvantages. Don't buy one that is tiny just for the sake of saving counter space; you will end up having to cook everything in batches, which is very annoying.

You will often need an air fryer of up to two litres for two to three people, and at least three litres if you're cooking for more. You may still find you need to batch cook, so definitely don't go for smaller! If you have the counter space, a large fryer is always going to be more flexible.

Breakfast Recipes

Savory French Toasts

Servings|2   Time|14 minutes

Nutritional Content (per serving):

Cal| 227   Fat| 3.3g   Protein| 7.7g   Carbs| 41.4g

Ingredients:

- 25 grams chickpea flour
- ¼ of green chili, seeded and finely chopped
- 1¼ grams ground cumin
- Water, as required
- 25 grams onion, finely chopped
- 2½ grams red chili powder
- 1¼ grams ground turmeric
- Salt, as required
- 4 bread slices

Directions:

1. Add all the Ingredients: except bread slices in a large bowl and mix until a thick mixture forms.
2. Spread the mixture over both sides of the bread slices.
3. Set the temperature of Air Fryer to 200 degrees C and preheat for 5 minutes. Line the Air Fryer pan with a piece of foil.
4. After preheating, arrange the bread slices in the prepared pan.
5. Slide the pan in Air Fryer and immediately set the temperature to 180 degrees C.
6. Set the time for 4 minutes.
7. Serve warm.

French Toast

Servings|2   Time|13 minutes

Nutritional Content (per serving):

Cal| 109   Fat| 1.5g   Protein| 10.5g   Carbs| 1.4g

Ingredients:

- ❖ 2 eggs
- ❖ 40 grams sugar
- ❖ Dash of vanilla extract
- ❖ 60 ml evaporated milk
- ❖ 10 milliliters olive oil
- ❖ 4 bread slices

Directions:

1. Set the temperature of Air Fryer to 160 degrees C and preheat for 5 minutes.
2. Grease an air fryer pan and insert in the Air Fryer while heating.
3. In a large bowl, mix together all Ingredients: except for bread slices.
4. Coat the bread slices with egg mixture evenly.
5. After preheating, arrange the bread slices into the prepared pan.
6. Slide the pan in Air Fryer and set the time for 6 minutes.
7. Flip the slices once after 3 minutes.
8. Serve warm.

Cheesy Toast with Egg & Bacon

Servings|4   Time|19 minutes

Nutritional Content (per serving):

Cal| 416   Fat| 29.3g   Protein| 27.2g   Carbs| 11.2g

Ingredients:

- ❖ 4 bread slices
- ❖ 113 grams ricotta cheese, crumbled
- ❖ Ground black pepper, as required
- ❖ 4 cooked bacon slices, crumbled
- ❖ 1 garlic clove, minced
- ❖ 1 gram lemon zest
- ❖ 2 hard-boiled eggs, peeled and chopped

Directions:

1. In a food processor, add the garlic, ricotta, lemon zest and black pepper and pulse until smooth.
2. Spread ricotta mixture over each bread slices evenly.
3. Set the temperature of Air Fryer to 180 degrees C and preheat for 5 minutes.
4. After preheating, arrange the bread slices into the greased air fryer basket.
5. Slide the basket in Air Fryer and set the time for 4 minutes.
6. Transfer the bread slices onto serving plates.
7. Top with egg and bacon pieces and serve.

Bacon & Egg Cups

Servings|2   Time|18 minutes

Nutritional Content (per serving):

Cal| 215   Fat| 11.4g   Protein| 14.9g   Carbs| 13.1g

Ingredients:

- ❖ 1 cooked bacon slice, chopped
- ❖ 30 milliliters milk
- ❖ 5 grams marinara sauce
- ❖ 1½ grams fresh parsley, chopped
- ❖ 2 eggs
- ❖ Ground black pepper, as required
- ❖ 10 grams Parmesan cheese, grated
- ❖ 2 bread slices, toasted and buttered

Directions:

1. Set the temperature of Air Fryer to 180 degrees C and preheat for 5 minutes.
2. Divide the bacon into 2 ramekins.
3. Crack 1 egg in each ramekin over the bacon.
4. Pour the milk over eggs and sprinkle with black pepper.
5. Top with marinara sauce, followed by the Parmesan cheese.
6. After preheating, arrange the ramekins into the air fryer basket.
7. Slide the basket in Air Fryer and set the time for 8 minutes.
8. Remove from Air Fryer and sprinkle with parsley.
9. Serve hot alongside the bread slices.

Cheese & Cream Omelet

Servings|2   Time|13 minutes

Nutritional Content (per serving):

Cal| 263   Fat| 20.4g   Protein| 15.8g   Carbs| 4.6g

Ingredients:

- ❖ 4 eggs
- ❖ Salt and ground black pepper, as required
- ❖ 60 grams cream
- ❖ 30 grams cheddar cheese, grated

Directions:

1. Lightly, grease a 6x3-inch baking pan.
2. In a bowl, add the eggs, cream, salt, and black pepper and beat until well combined.
3. Place the egg mixture into the prepared pan.
4. Set the temperature of Air Fryer to 175 degrees C and preheat for 5 minutes.
5. After preheating, arrange the baking pan into Air Fryer basket.
6. Slide the basket in Air Fryer and set the time for 8 minutes.
7. After 4 minutes of cooking, sprinkle the cheese on the top of omelet.
8. Transfer the omelet onto a plate.
9. Cut in 2 portions and serve hot.

Sausage & Bacon Omelet

Servings|2   Time|20 minutes

Nutritional Content (per serving):

Cal| 500   Fat| 38.4g   Protein| 33.2g   Carbs| 6g

Ingredients:

- ❖ 4 eggs
- ❖ 2 sausages, chopped
- ❖ 1 bacon slice, chopped
- ❖ 1 yellow onion, chopped

Directions:

1. In a bowl, whip the eggs well.
2. Add the remaining Ingredients: and gently, stir to combine.
3. Place the mixture into a baking pan.
4. Set the temperature of Air Fryer to 160 degrees C and preheat for 5 minutes.
5. After preheating, arrange the baking pan in air fryer basket.
6. Slide the basket in Air Fryer and set the time for 10 minutes.
7. Transfer the omelet onto a plate.
8. Cut into equal-sized wedges and serve hot.

Salmon Quiche

Servings|2   Time|30 minutes

Nutritional Content (per serving):

Cal| 596   Fat| 39.1g   Protein| 27.2g   Carbs| 34.4g

Ingredients:

- 155 grams salmon fillet, chopped
- 10 milliliters fresh lemon juice
- 1 egg yolk
- 85 grams flour
- 2 eggs
- 1 scallion, chopped
- Salt and ground black pepper, as required
- 50 grams chilled butter
- 20 milliliters cold water
- 45 grams whipping cream

Directions:

1. In a bowl, mix together the salmon, salt, black pepper and lemon juice. Set aside.
2. In another bowl, add egg yolk, butter, flour and water and mix until a dough forms.
3. Place the dough onto a floured smooth surface and roll into about 7-inch round.
4. Place the dough in a quiche pan and press firmly in the bottom and along the edges. Trim the excess edges.
5. In a small bowl, add the eggs, cream, salt and black pepper and beat until well combined.
6. Place the cream mixture over crust evenly and top with the chopped salmon, followed by the scallion.
7. Set the temperature of Air Fryer to 180 degrees C and preheat for 5 minutes.
8. After preheating, arrange the quiche pan into Air Fryer basket.
9. Slide the basket in Air Fryer and set the time for 20 minutes.

10. Remove the pan from Air Fryer and place onto a wire rack to cool for about 5 minutes before serving.

Veggies Frittata

Servings|2   Time|30 minutes

Nutritional Content (per serving):

Cal| 278   Fat| 19.4g   Protein| 18.8g   Carbs| 8g

Ingredients:

- ❖ 60 grams half-and-half
- ❖ Salt and ground black pepper, as required
- ❖ 50 grams tomato, chopped
- ❖ 4 large eggs
- ❖ 60 grams fresh spinach, chopped
- ❖ 60 grams onion, chopped
- ❖ 55 grams feta cheese, crumbled

Directions:

1. In a bowl, add the half-and-half, eggs, salt and black pepper and beat until well combined.
2. Add the spinach, onion, tomatoes and feta cheese and mix well.
3. Place the mixture into a baking pan.
4. Set the temperature of Air Fryer to 185 degrees C and preheat for 5 minutes.
5. After preheating, arrange the baking pan into Air Fryer basket.
6. Slide the basket in Air Fryer and set the time for 18 minutes.
7. Remove the pan from Air Fryer and place onto a wire rack to cool for about 5 minutes before serving.

Sausage & Capsicum Casserole

Servings|6   Time|40 minutes

Nutritional Content (per serving):

Cal| 391   Fat| 31.1g   Protein| 24.4g   Carbs| 2.5g

Ingredients:

- ❖ 5 milliliters olive oil
- ❖ 455 grams ground sausage
- ❖ 30 grams onion, chopped
- ❖ 55 grams Colby Jack cheese, shredded
- ❖ 2½ grams garlic salt
- ❖ 1 capsicum, seeded and chopped
- ❖ 8 eggs, beaten
- ❖ 5 grams fennel seed

Directions:

1. In a skillet, heat the oil over medium heat and cook the sausage for about 4-5 minutes.
2. Add the capsicum and onion and cook for about 4-5 minutes.
3. Remove from the heat and transfer the sausage mixture into a bowl to cool slightly.
4. In a baking pan, place the sausage mixture and top with the cheese, followed by the beaten eggs, fennel seed and garlic salt.
5. Set the temperature of Air Fryer to 200 degrees C and preheat for 5 minutes.
6. After preheating, arrange the baking pan into the air fryer basket.
7. Slide the basket in Air Fryer and set the time for 15 minutes.
8. Cut into equal-sized wedges and serve hot.

Oat & Raisin Muffins

Servings|4   Time|24 minutes

Nutritional Content (per serving):

Cal| 409   Fat| 25.7g   Protein| 5.8g   Carbs| 40.6g

Ingredient

- ❖ 65 grams flour
- ❖ ½ gram baking powder
- ❖ 113 grams butter, softened
- ❖ 1¼ milliliters vanilla extract
- ❖ 25 grams rolled oats
- ❖ 65 grams powdered sugar
- ❖ 2 eggs
- ❖ 37½ grams raisins

Directions:

1. In a bowl, mix together the flour, oats, and baking powder.
2. In another bowl, add the sugar and butter. Beat until you get the creamy texture.
3. Then, add in the egg and vanilla extract and beat until well combined.
4. Add the egg mixture into oat mixture and mix until just combined.
5. Fold in the raisins.
6. Set the temperature of Air Fryer to 180 degrees C and preheat for 5 minutes.
7. Place the mixture into 4 greased muffin molds evenly.
8. After preheating, arrange the molds into the air fryer basket.
9. Slide the basket in Air Fryer and set the time for 10 minutes.
10. Place the molds onto a wire rack to cool for about 10 minutes.
11. Carefully invert the muffins onto the wire rack to completely cool before serving.

Banana Muffins

Servings|4   Time|20 minutes

Nutritional Content (per serving):

Cal| 229   Fat| 14g   Protein| 3g   Carbs| 24.6g

Ingredients:

- ❖ 25 grams oats
- ❖ 2 grams baking powder
- ❖ 55 grams unsalted butter, softened
- ❖ 5 milliliters milk
- ❖ 35 grams refined flour
- ❖ 35 grams powdered sugar
- ❖ 75 grams banana, peeled and mashed
- ❖ 15 grams walnuts, chopped

Directions:

1. In a bowl, mix together the oats, flour and baking powder.
2. In another bowl, add the sugar and butter and beat until creamy
3. Add the banana and vanilla extract and beat until well combined.
4. Add the flour mixture and milk in banana mixture and mix until just combined.
5. Fold in the walnuts.
6. Place the mixture into 4 greased muffin molds evenly.
7. Set the temperature of Air Fryer to 160 degrees C and preheat for 5 minutes.
8. After preheating, arrange the muffin molds into Air Fryer basket.
9. Slide the basket in Air Fryer and set the time for 10 minutes.
10. Remove the muffin molds from Air Fryer and place onto a wire rack to cool for about 10 minutes.
11. Carefully, invert the muffins onto the wire rack to completely cool before serving.

Apple Muffins

Servings|12   Time|35 minutes

Nutritional Content (per serving):

Cal| 110   Fat| 0.2g   Protein| 2.1g   Carbs| 25.3g

Ingredients:

- 230 grams plain flour
- 6 grams baking powder
- 1¼ grams ground ginger
- 95 grams applesauce

- 75 grams sugar
- 2½ grams ground cinnamon
- 1¼ grams salt
- 120 grams apple, cored and chopped

Directions:

1. In a large bowl, mix together the flour, sugar, baking powder, spices, and salt.
2. Add in the milk and applesauce. Beat until just combined.
3. Fold in the chopped apple.
4. Set the temperature of Air Fryer to 200 degrees C and preheat for 5 minutes.
5. Put the mixture evenly into 12 greased muffin molds.
6. After preheating, arrange the molds into an Air Fryer basket.
7. Slide the basket in Air Fryer and set the time for 25 minutes.
8. Remove the muffin molds from Air Fryer and place onto a wire rack to cool for about 10 minutes.
9. Carefully, invert the muffins onto the wire rack to completely cool before serving.

Zucchini Bread

Servings|16   Time|35 minutes

Nutritional Content (per serving):

Cal| 367   Fat| 18.6g   Protein| 5.2g   Carbs| 47.4g

Ingredients:

- ❖ 360 grams all-purpose flour
- ❖ 4 grams baking soda
- ❖ 5 grams salt
- ❖ 240 milliliters vegetable oil
- ❖ 15 milliliters vanilla extract
- ❖ 100 grams walnuts, chopped

- ❖ 4 grams baking powder
- ❖ 10 grams ground cinnamon
- ❖ 450 grams sugar
- ❖ 3 eggs
- ❖ 350 grams zucchini, grated

Directions:

1. In a bowl, and mix together the flour, baking powder, baking soda, cinnamon, and salt.
2. In another large bowl, add the sugar, oil, eggs, and vanilla extract. Beat until well combined.
3. Then, add in the flour mixture and stir until just combined.
4. Gently, fold in the zucchini and walnuts.
5. Set the temperature of Air Fryer to 160 degrees C and preheat for 5 minutes.
6. Grease and flour 2 (8x4-inch) loaf pans.
7. Place the mixture into the prepared pans evenly.
8. After preheating, arrange the loaf pans into an Air Fryer basket.
9. Slide the basket in Air Fryer and set the time for 20 minutes.
10. Remove the pans from Air Fryer and place onto a wire rack for about 10-15 minutes.
11. Carefully, remove the breads from each pan and place onto the wire rack to cool completely before slicing.
12. Cut each bread into desired sized slices and serve.

Banana Bread

Servings|8   Time|30 minutes

Nutritional Content (per serving):

Cal| 301   Fat| 14.9.g   Protein| 3.6g   Carbs| 41.1g

Ingredient

- ❖ 200 grams flour
- ❖ 4 grams baking soda
- ❖ 5 grams ground cinnamon
- ❖ 120 milliliters milk
- ❖ 3 bananas, peeled and sliced
- ❖ 85 grams sugar
- ❖ 4 grams baking powder
- ❖ 5 grams salt
- ❖ 120 milliliter olive oil

Directions:

1. In a bowl of a stand mixer, add all the Ingredients: and mix well.
2. Place the mixture into a greased loaf pan.
3. Set the temperature of air fryer to 165 degrees C and preheat for 5 minutes.
4. After preheating, arrange the loaf pan into the air fryer basket.
5. Slide the basket in Air Fryer and set the time for 20 minutes.
6. Remove from air fryer and place the pan onto a wire rack for about 10-15 minutes.
7. Carefully invert the bread onto a wire rack to cool completely before slicing.
8. Cut the bread into desired sized slices and serve.

Cream Bread

Servings|12   Time|1 hour

Nutritional Content (per serving):

Cal| 262   Fat| 5.6g   Protein| 8.8g   Carbs| 42.5g

Ingredients:

- ❖ 240 milliliters milk
- ❖ 1 large egg
- ❖ 60 grams all-purpose flour
- ❖ 5 grams salt
- ❖ 15 grams dry yeast
- ❖ 180 grams whipping cream
- ❖ 540 grams bread flour
- ❖ 15 grams milk powder
- ❖ 50 grams fine sugar

Directions:

1. In the baking pan of a bread machine, place all the Ingredients: in the order recommended by the manufacturer.
2. Place the baking pan in bread machine and close with the lid.
3. Select the Dough cycle and press Start button.
4. Once the cycle is completed, remove the paddles from bread machine but keep the dough inside for about 45-50 minutes to proof.
5. Grease 2 loaf pans.
6. Remove the dough from pan and place onto a lightly floured surface.
7. Divide the dough into four equal-sized balls and then, roll each into a rectangle.
8. Tightly, roll each rectangle like a Swiss roll.
9. Place two rolls into each prepared loaf pan. Set aside for about 1 hour.
10. Set the temperature of Air Fryer to 190 degrees C and preheat for 5 minutes.
11. After preheating, arrange the loaf pans into an Air Fryer basket.
12. Slide the basket in Air Fryer and set the time for 50-55 minutes.
13. Remove the pans from Air Fryer and place onto a wire rack for about 10-15 minutes.
14. Then, remove the bread rolls from pans and place onto a wire rack until they are completely cool before slicing.
15. Cut each roll into desired size slices and serve.

Poultry Recipes

Herbed Cornish Game Hen

Servings|4   Time|31 minutes

Nutritional Content (per serving):

Cal| 698   Fat| 61.1g   Protein| 38.7g   Carbs| 2g

Ingredients:

- ❖ 120 milliliters olive oil
- ❖ 1½ grams fresh thyme, chopped
- ❖ 1½ grams fresh lemon zest, grated
- ❖ 910 grams Cornish game hen, backbone removed and halved
- ❖ 1½ grams fresh rosemary, chopped
- ❖ 5 grams sugar
- ❖ 1¼ grams red pepper flakes
- ❖ Salt and ground black pepper, as required

Directions:

1. In a bowl, mix together oil, herbs, lemon zest, sugar, and spices.
2. Add the hen portions and generously coat with the marinade.
3. Cover and refrigerate for about 24 hours.
4. In a strainer, place the hen portions and set aside to drain any liquid.
5. Set the temperature of Air Fryer to 200 degrees C and preheat for 5 minutes.
6. After preheating, arrange the hen portions into the greased Air Fryer basket.
7. Slide the basket in Air Fryer and set the time for 16 minutes.
8. Transfer the hen portions onto serving plates and serve.

Simple Whole Chicken

Servings|2   Time|50 minutes

Nutritional Content (per serving):

Cal| 698   Fat| 49.6g   Protein| 63.8g   Carbs| 0g

Ingredient

- ❖ 1 (680-grams) whole chicken
- ❖ 15 millimeters olive oil
- ❖ Salt and ground black pepper, as required

Directions:

1. Set the temperature of Air Fryer to 200 degrees C and preheat for 5 minutes.
2. Season the chicken with salt and black pepper.
3. After preheating, place the chicken into the greased air fryer basket.
4. Slide the basket in Air Fryer and set the time for 35-40 minutes or until done completely.
5. Remove from the Air Fryer and place the chicken onto a platter.
6. With a sharp knife, cut the chicken into desired sized pieces and serve.

Spiced Whole Chicken

Servings|6   Time|1¼ hours

Nutritional Content (per serving):

Cal| 781   Fat| 54.4g   Protein| 67.7g   Carbs| 3.5g

Ingredients:

- 1½ grams dried thyme
- 5 grams cayenne pepper
- 5 grams onion powder
- Salt and ground black pepper, as required
- 45 milliliters olive oil
- 10 grams paprika
- 5 grams ground white pepper
- 5 grams garlic powder
- 1 (2¼-kilogram) whole chicken, necks and giblets removed

Directions:

1. In a bowl, mix together the thyme and spices.
2. Generously, coat the chicken with oil and then rub it with spice mixture.
3. Set the temperature of Air Fryer to 175 degrees C and preheat for 5 minutes.
4. After preheating, arrange the chicken into the greased Air Fryer basket, breast side down.
5. Slide the basket in Air Fryer and set the time for 30 minutes.
6. Flip the chicken and immediately set the time for 30 more minutes.
7. Remove from the Air Fryer and place chicken onto a cutting board for about 10 minutes before carving.
8. Slice the chicken into desired size pieces and serve.

Spicy Chicken Legs

Servings|4   Time|30 minutes

Nutritional Content (per serving):

Cal| 507   Fat| 18.9g   Protein| 19.6g   Carbs| 2.8g

Ingredient

- ❖ 4 chicken legs
- ❖ 2 grams fresh ginger, minced
- ❖ Salt, as required
- ❖ 10 grams red chili powder
- ❖ Ground black pepper, as required

- ❖ 45 milliliters fresh lemon juice
- ❖ 2 grams garlic, minced
- ❖ 60 grams plain Greek yogurt
- ❖ 5 grams ground cumin

Directions:

1. In a bowl, mix together the chicken legs, lemon juice, ginger, garlic and salt. Set aside for about 15 minutes.
2. Meanwhile, in another bowl, mix together the yogurt and spices.
3. Add the chicken legs and coat with the spice mixture generously.
4. Cover the bowl and refrigerate for at least 10-12 hours.
5. Set the temperature of Air Fryer to 230 degrees C and preheat for 5 minutes.
6. Line the Air fryer basket with a piece of foil.
7. After preheating, arrange chicken legs into the prepared air fryer basket.
8. Slide the basket in Air Fryer and set the time for 18-20 minutes.
9. Serve hot.

Crispy Chicken Legs

Servings|3   Time|30 minutes

Nutritional Content (per serving):

Cal| 599   Fat| 31.7g   Protein| 43.4g   Carbs| 38.2g

Ingredients:

- 3 (225-gram) chicken legs
- 130 grams white flour
- 5 grams onion powder
- 5 grams paprika
- 15 milliliters olive oil
- 240 milliliters buttermilk
- 5 grams garlic powder
- 5 grams ground cumin
- Salt and ground black pepper, as required

Directions:

1. In a bowl, place the chicken legs and buttermilk and refrigerate for about 2 hours.
2. In a shallow dish, mix together the flour and spices.
3. Remove the chicken from buttermilk.
4. Coat the chicken legs with flour mixture, then dip into buttermilk and finally, coat with the flour mixture again.
5. Drizzle the chicken legs with the oil.
6. Set the temperature of Air Fryer to 185 degrees C and preheat for 5 minutes.
7. After preheating, arrange the chicken legs into the greased Air Fryer basket.
8. Slide the basket in Air Fryer and set the time for 20 minutes.
9. Transfer the chicken legs onto serving plates and serve hot.

Glazed Chicken Drumsticks

Servings|4   Time|37 minutes

Nutritional Content (per serving):

Cal| 292   Fat| 18.6g   Protein| 25.1g   Carbs| 5.8g

Ingredients:

- 80 grams Dijon mustard
- 30 milliliters olive oil
- 2 grams fresh thyme, minced
- 4 (150-grams) boneless chicken drumsticks
- 15 grams honey
- 1 gram fresh rosemary, minced
- Salt and ground black pepper, as required

Directions:

1. In a bowl, add the mustard, honey, oil, herbs, salt, and black pepper and mix well.
2. Add the drumsticks and coat with the mixture generously.
3. Cover and refrigerate to marinate overnight.
4. Set the temperature of Air Fryer to 160 degrees C and preheat for 5 minutes.
5. After preheating, arrange the chicken drumsticks into the greased air fryer basket in a single layer.
6. Slide the basket in Air Fryer and set the time for 12 minutes.
7. After 12 minutes of cooking, set the temperature of Air Fryer to 180 degrees C for 5-10 more minutes.
8. Serve hot.

Gingered Chicken Drumsticks

Servings|3   Time|35 minutes

Nutritional Content (per serving):

Cal| 344   Fat| 14.2g   Protein| 47.5g   Carbs| 3.8g

Ingredients:

- ❖ 60 milliliters full-fat coconut milk
- ❖ 10 grams ground turmeric
- ❖ 3 (170-gram) chicken drumsticks
- ❖ 3½ grams fresh ginger, minced
- ❖ 3½ grams fresh galangal, minced
- ❖ Salt, as required

Directions:

1. In a bowl, mix together the coconut milk, galangal, ginger, and spices.
2. Add the chicken drumsticks and generously coat with the marinade.
3. Refrigerate to marinate for at least 6-8 hours.
4. Set the temperature of Air Fryer to 190 degrees C and preheat for 5 minutes.
5. After preheating, arrange the chicken drumsticks into the greased Air Fryer basket in a single layer.
6. Slide the basket in Air Fryer and set the time for 20-25 minutes.
7. Transfer the chicken drumsticks onto a serving platter and serve hot.

Lemony Chicken Thighs

Servings|6   Time|30 minutes

Nutritional Content (per serving):

Cal| 367   Fat| 17.5g   Protein| 49.3g   Carbs| 0.4g

Ingredients:

- ❖ 6 (170-gram) chicken thighs
- ❖ 30 milliliters fresh lemon juice
- ❖ Salt and ground black pepper, as required
- ❖ 30 milliliters olive oil
- ❖ 3 grams Italian seasoning
- ❖ 1 lemon, sliced thinly

Directions:

1. In a large bowl, add all the Ingredients: except for lemon slices and toss to coat well.
2. Refrigerate to marinate for 30 minutes to overnight.
3. Remove the chicken thighs and let any excess marinade drip off.
4. Set the temperature of Air Fryer to 175 degrees C and preheat for 5 minutes.
5. After preheating, arrange the chicken thighs into the greased Air Fryer basket.
6. Slide the basket in Air Fryer and set the time for 20 minutes.
7. After 10 minutes of cooking, flip the chicken thighs.
8. Transfer the chicken thighs onto serving plates and serve hot alongside the lemon slices.

Oat Crusted Chicken Breasts

Servings|2 Time|27 minutes

Nutritional Content (per serving):

Cal| 429   Fat| 13.8g   Protein| 45.1g   Carbs| 29.8g

Ingredient

- ❖ 2 (150-grams) chicken breasts
- ❖ 75 grams oats
- ❖ 2 grams fresh parsley
- ❖ 2 medium eggs
- ❖ Salt and ground black pepper, as required
- ❖ 20-30 grams mustard powder

Directions:

1. Place the chicken breasts onto a cutting board and with a meat mallet; flatten each into an even thickness.
2. Then, cut each breast in half. Sprinkle the chicken breasts with salt and black pepper and set aside.
3. In a blender, add the oats, mustard powder, parsley, salt and black pepper and pulse until a coarse breadcrumb like mixture is formed.
4. Transfer the oat mixture into a shallow bowl.
5. In another bowl, crack the eggs and beat well.
6. Coat the chicken breasts with oat mixture and then dip into beaten eggs and again coat with the oats mixture.
7. Set the temperature of Air Fryer to 175 degrees C and preheat for 5 minutes.
8. Aster preheating, arrange chicken breasts onto the greased grill pan in a single layer.
9. Slide the grill pan in Air Fryer and set the time for 12 minutes.
10. Flip the chicken breasts once halfway through.
11. Serve hot.

Parmesan Chicken Breast

Servings|3   Time|40 minutes

Nutritional Content (per serving):

Cal| 593   Fat| 26.5g   Protein| 59.1g   Carbs| 28.2g

Ingredients:

- ❖ 3 (170-gram) chicken breasts
- ❖ 115 grams breadcrumbs
- ❖ 30 milliliters vegetable oil
- ❖ 30 grams Parmesan cheese, grated
- ❖ 1 egg, beaten
- ❖ 3½ grams fresh basil
- ❖ 55 grams pasta sauce

Directions:

1. In a shallow bowl, beat the egg.
2. In another bowl, add the oil, breadcrumbs, and basil and mix until a crumbly mixture forms.
3. Now, dip each chicken breast into the beaten egg and then, coat with the breadcrumb mixture.
4. Set the temperature of Air Fryer to 175 degrees C and preheat for 5 minutes.
5. After preheating, arrange chicken breasts into the greased basket.
6. Slide the basket in Air Fryer and set the time for 20 minutes.
7. After 15 minutes of cooking, spoon the pasta sauce over chicken breasts evenly and sprinkle with cheese.
8. Transfer the chicken breasts onto a serving platter and serve hot.

Bacon-Wrapped Chicken Breasts

Servings|4   Time|38 minutes

Nutritional Content (per serving):

Cal| 365   Fat| 24.9g   Protein| 30.2g   Carbs| 2.7g

Ingredient

- ❖ 10 grams palm sugar
- ❖ 30 milliliters fish sauce
- ❖ 2 (226-grams) chicken breasts, cut each breast in half horizontally
- ❖ 10 grams honey
- ❖ 6-7 Fresh basil leaves
- ❖ 30 milliliters water
- ❖ Salt and ground black pepper, as required
- ❖ 12 bacon strips

Directions:

1. In a small heavy-bottomed pan, add palm sugar over medium-low heat and cook for about 2-3 minutes or until caramelized, stirring continuously.
2. Add the basil, fish sauce and water and stir to combine.
3. Remove from heat and transfer the sugar mixture into a large bowl.
4. Sprinkle each chicken breast with salt and black pepper.
5. Add the chicken pieces into the bowl of sugar mixture and coat well.
6. Refrigerate to marinate for about 4-6 hours.
7. Wrap each chicken piece with 3 bacon strips.
8. Coat each piece with honey slightly.
9. Set the temperature of Air Fryer to 185 degrees C and preheat for 5 minutes.
10. Arrange the chicken pieces into the greased air fryer basket.
11. Slide the basket in Air Fryer and set the time for 20 minutes.
12. Flip the chicken pieces once halfway through.
13. Serve hot.

Simple Turkey Breast

Servings|10   Time|55 minutes

Nutritional Content (per serving):

Cal| 720   Fat| 9g   Protein| 97.2g   Carbs| 0g

Ingredient

- ❖ 1 (3 kilograms 640 grams) bone-in turkey breast
- ❖ 30 milliliters olive oil
- ❖ Salt and ground black pepper, as required

Directions:

1. Set the temperature of Air Fryer to 180 degrees C and preheat for 5 minutes.
2. Sprinkle the turkey breast with salt and black pepper and drizzle with oil.
3. After preheating, arrange turkey breast into the greased air fryer basket, skin side down.
4. Slide the basket in Air Fryer and set the time for 45 minutes.
5. After 20 minutes of cooking, flip the turkey breast.
6. Remove from Air Fryer and place the turkey breast onto a cutting board for about 10 minutes before slicing.
7. With a sharp knife, cut the turkey breast into desired sized slices and serve.

Herbed Turkey Breast

Servings|6   Time|45 minutes

Nutritional Content (per serving):

Cal| 349   Fat| 16g   Protein| 40.7g   Carbs| 1.8g

Ingredients:

- ❖ 1½ grams dried rosemary, crushed
- ❖ 5 grams dark brown sugar
- ❖ 2½ grams paprika
- ❖ 15 milliliters olive oil

- ❖ 1½ grams dried sage, crushed
- ❖ 2½ grams garlic powder
- ❖ 1 (1135-gram) bone-in, skin-on turkey breast

- ❖ 1½ grams dried thyme, crushed

Directions:

1. In a bowl, mix together the herbs, brown sugar, and spices.
2. Coat the turkey breast evenly with oil and then, generously rub with the herb mixture.
3. Set the temperature of Air Fryer to 185 degrees C and preheat for 5 minutes.
4. After preheating, arrange the turkey breast into the greased Air Fryer basket, skin-side down.
5. Slide the basket in Air Fryer and set the time for 35 minutes.
6. Flip the turkey breast once halfway through.
7. Place the turkey breast onto a cutting board for about 10 minutes before slicing.
8. With a sharp knife, cut the turkey breast into desired size slices and serve.

Zesty Turkey Legs

Servings|2   Time|45 minutes

Nutritional Content (per serving):

Cal| 458   Fat| 29.5g   Protein| 44.6g   Carbs| 2.3g

Ingredients:

- ❖ 2 garlic cloves, minced
- ❖ 3 grams fresh lime zest, finely grated
- ❖ 15 milliliters fresh lime juice
- ❖ 2 turkey legs
- ❖ 2 grams fresh rosemary, minced
- ❖ 30 milliliters olive oil
- ❖ Salt and ground black pepper, as required

Directions:

1. In a large bowl, mix together the garlic, rosemary, lime zest, oil, lime juice, salt, and black pepper.
2. Add the turkey legs and generously coat with marinade.
3. Refrigerate to marinate for about 6-8 hours.
4. Set the temperature of Air Fryer to 175 degrees C and preheat for 5 minutes.
5. After preheating, arrange the turkey legs into the greased air fryer basket.
6. Slide the basket in Air Fryer and set the time for 30 minutes.
7. Flip the turkey legs once halfway through.
8. Serve hot.

Turkey Meatloaf

Servings|4   Time|35 minutes

Nutritional Content (per serving):

Cal| 429   Fat| 18g   Protein| 36.9g   Carbs| 33.5g

Ingredients:

- 455 grams ground turkey
- 52 grams onion, chopped
- 1 (113-gram) can chopped green chilies
- 1 egg, beaten
- 115 grams Monterey Jack cheese, grated
- 5 grams fresh Coriander, chopped
- 2½ grams ground cumin
- Salt and ground black pepper, as required
- 55 grams fresh kale, trimmed and finely chopped
- 2 garlic cloves, minced
- 50 grams fresh breadcrumbs
- 65 grams salsa verde
- 5 grams red chili powder
- 2½ grams dried oregano, crushed

Directions:

1. In a deep bowl, place all the Ingredients: and with your hands, mix until well combined.
2. Divide the turkey mixture into 4 equal-sized portions and shape each into a mini loaf.
3. Set the temperature of Air Fryer to 205 degrees C and preheat for 5 minutes.
4. After preheating, arrange the loaves into the greased air fryer basket.
5. Slide the basket in Air Fryer and set the time for 20 minutes.
6. Remove from air fryer and place the loaves onto plates for about 5 minutes before serving.
7. Serve warm.

Red Meat Recipes

Spicy Round Roast

Servings|8   Time|1 hour

Nutritional Content (per serving):

Cal| 29   Fat| 12.5g   Protein| 43.2g   Carbs| 0.9g

Ingredients:

- ❖ 1135 grams beef round roast, trimmed
- ❖ 2½ grams garlic powder
- ❖ 2½ grams ground black pepper
- ❖ 30 milliliters olive oil
- ❖ 2½ grams onion powder
- ❖ 2½ grams cayenne pepper
- ❖ Salt, as required

Directions:

1. In a bowl, mix together the oil and spices.
2. Coat the roast with spice mixture evenly.
3. Set the temperature of Air Fryer to 185 degrees C and preheat for 5 minutes.
4. After preheating, arrange the roast in greased Air Fryer basket.
5. Slide the basket in Air Fryer and set the time for 50 minutes.
6. Transfer the roast onto a platter and with a piece of foil, cover for about 10 minutes before slicing.
7. Cut the roast into desired sized slices and serve.

Bacon-Wrapped Filet Mignon

Servings|2   Time|25 minutes

Nutritional Content (per serving):

Cal| 428   Fat| 22.3g   Protein| 52.9g   Carbs| 0.5g

Ingredients:

- 2 bacon slices
- Salt and ground black pepper, as required
- 2 (150-grams) filet mignon steaks
- 5 milliliters avocado oil

Directions:

1. Wrap 1 bacon slice around each mignon steak and secure with a toothpick.
2. Season the steak evenly with salt and black pepper.
3. Then, coat each steak with avocado oil.
4. Set the temperature of Air Fryer to 190 degrees C and preheat for 5 minutes.
5. After preheating, arrange the mignon steaks into the greased air fryer basket.
6. Slide the basket in Air Fryer and set the time for 15 minutes.
7. Flip the mignon steaks once halfway through.
8. Serve hot.

Buttered Rib-Eye Steak

Servings|4   Time|29 minutes

Nutritional Content (per serving):

Cal| 459   Fat| 36.5g   Protein| 31.2g   Carbs| 0.9g

Ingredients:

- 113 grams unsalted butter, softened
- 4 grams garlic, minced
- Salt, as required
- Ground black pepper, as required
- 3 grams fresh parsley, chopped
- 5 milliliters Worcestershire sauce
- 2 (226-grams) rib-eye steaks
- 15 milliliters olive oil

Directions:

1. In a bowl, add the butter, parsley, garlic, Worcestershire sauce, and salt and mix until well combined.
2. Place the butter mixture onto parchment paper and roll into a log.
3. Refrigerate until using.
4. Coat the steak evenly with oil and then sprinkle with salt and black pepper.
5. Set the temperature of Air Fryer to 205 degrees C and preheat for 5 minutes.
6. After preheating, arrange the steaks into the greased air fryer basket.
7. Slide the basket in Air Fryer and set the time for 14 minutes.
8. Flip the steaks once halfway through.
9. Place the steaks onto a platter for about 5 minutes.
10. Cut each steak into desired sized slices and divide onto serving plates.
11. Now, cut the butter log into slices.
12. Top steak slices with butter slices and serve.

Crumbed Sirloin Steak

Servings|4   Time|20 minutes

Nutritional Content (per serving):

Cal| 454   Fat| 10.6g   Protein| 37.2g   Carbs| 31.8g

Ingredients:

- ❖ 130 grams white flour
- ❖ 120 grams panko breadcrumbs
- ❖ 5 grams onion powder
- ❖ Salt and ground black pepper, as required

- ❖ 2 eggs
- ❖ 5 grams garlic powder
- ❖ 2½ grams paprika
- ❖ 4 (170-gram) sirloin steaks, pounded slightly

Directions:

1. In a shallow bowl, place the flour.
2. Crack the eggs in a second bowl and beat well.
3. In a third bowl, mix together the panko and spices.
4. Coat each steak with the flour, then dip into beaten eggs and finally, coat with panko mixture.
5. Set the temperature of Air Fryer to 185 degrees C and preheat for 5 minutes.
6. After preheating, arrange the steaks into Air Fryer basket.
7. Slide the basket in Air Fryer and set the time for 10 minutes.
8. Transfer the steaks onto the serving plates and serve immediately.

Smoky Beef Burgers

Servings|4   Time|25 minutes

Nutritional Content (per serving):

Cal| 220   Fat| 7.1g   Protein| 34.7g   Carbs| 1.8g

Ingredients:

- 455 grams ground beef
- 5 grams Maggi seasoning sauce
- 3-4 drops liquid smoke
- 2½ grams garlic powder
- Olive oil cooking spray
- 15 milliliters Worcestershire sauce
- 1½ grams dried parsley
- Salt and ground black pepper, as required

Directions:

1. In a large bowl, mix together the beef, sauces, liquid smoke, parsley, and spices.
2. Make 4 equal-sized patties from the mixture.
3. Set the temperature of Air Fryer to 175 degrees C and preheat for 5 minutes.
4. Grease an Air Fryer pan.
5. After preheating, arrange the patties into the prepared pan in a single layer.
6. With your thumb, make an indent in the center of each patty and spray with cooking spray.
7. Slide the pan in Air Fryer and set the time for 10 minutes.
8. Serve hot.

Glazed Pork Shoulder

Servings|5   Time|33 minutes

Nutritional Content (per serving):

Cal| 507   Fat| 36.9g   Protein| 31.7g   Carbs| 9.7g

Ingredients:

- ❖ 90 milliliters soy sauce
- ❖ 907 grams pork shoulder, cut into 3¾-centimeters thick slices
- ❖ 5 grams sugar
- ❖ 15 grams honey

Directions:

1. In a bowl, mix together the soy sauce, sugar, and honey.
2. Add the pork and coat with marinade generously.
3. Cover the bowl and refrigerate to marinate for about 4-6 hours.
4. Set the temperature of Air Fryer to 180 degrees C and preheat for 5 minutes.
5. After preheating, arrange the pork shoulder into the greased air fryer basket.
6. Slide the basket in Air Fryer and set the time for 10 minutes.
7. After 10 minutes of cooking, set the temperature of Air fryer to 200 degrees C for 8 minutes.
8. Transfer the pork shoulder onto a platter and with a piece of foil, cover for about 10 minutes before slicing.
9. Cut the pork shoulder into desired sized slices and serve.

Glazed Pork Tenderloin

Servings|3   Time|35 minutes

Nutritional Content (per serving):

Cal| 263   Fat| 5.3g   Protein| 39.7g   Carbs| 11.7g

Ingredients:

- ❖ 455 grams pork tenderloin
- ❖ 35 grams honey
- ❖ 30 milliliters Sriracha
- ❖ Salt, as required

Directions:

1. In a small bowl, add the Sriracha, honey and salt and mix well.
2. Brush the pork tenderloin with honey mixture evenly.
3. Set the temperature of Air Fryer to 175 degrees C and preheat for 5 minutes.
4. After preheating, arrange the pork tenderloin into the greased Air Fryer basket.
5. Slide the basket in Air Fryer and set the time for 25 minutes.
6. Place the pork tenderloin onto a platter for about 10 minutes before slicing.
7. With a sharp knife, cut the roast into desired sized slices and serve.

Breaded Pork Chops

Servings|2   Time|25 minutes

Nutritional Content (per serving):

Cal| 567   Fat| 22g   Protein| 38.8g   Carbs| 54.7g

Ingredients:

- 2 (150-grams) pork chops
- 32½ grams plain flour
- 113 grams breadcrumbs
- 15 milliliters vegetable oil
- Salt and ground black pepper, as required
- 1 egg

Directions:

1. Season each pork chop evenly with salt and pepper.
2. In a shallow bowl, place the flour.
3. In a second bowl, crack the egg and beat well.
4. In a third bowl, add the breadcrumbs and oil and mix until a crumbly mixture forms.
5. Coat the pork chop with flour, then dip into beaten egg and finally, coat with the breadcrumb mixture.
6. Set the temperature of Air Fryer to 205 degrees C and preheat for 5 minutes.
7. After preheating, arrange the chops into the greased air fryer basket.
8. Slide the basket in Air Fryer and set the time for 15 minutes.
9. Flip the chops once halfway through.
10. Serve hot.

BBQ Pork Chops

Servings|6   Time|26 minutes

Nutritional Content (per serving):

Cal| 346   Fat| 15.9g   Protein| 38.4g   Carbs| 8.3g

Ingredients:

- ❖ 6 (225-gram) pork loin chops
- ❖ 115 grams BBQ sauce

- ❖ Salt and ground black pepper, as required

Directions:

1. With a meat mallet, pound the chops completely.
2. Sprinkle the chops with a little salt and black pepper.
3. In a large bowl, add the BBQ sauce and chops and mix well.
4. Refrigerate, covered for about 6-8 hours.
5. Remove the chops from bowl and discard the excess sauce.
6. Set the temperature of Air Fryer to 180 degrees C and preheat for 5 minutes.
7. After preheating, arrange the pork chops into the greased Air Fryer basket.
8. Slide the basket in Air Fryer and set the time for 16 minutes.
9. Flip the chops once halfway through.
10. Serve hot.

Glazed Ham

Servings|4   Time|55 minutes

Nutritional Content (per serving):

Cal| 515   Fat| 17.8g   Protein| 32.6g   Carbs| 17.9g

Ingredients:

- ❖ 752 grams ham
- ❖ 30 grams French mustard
- ❖ 240 grams whiskey
- ❖ 25 grams honey

Directions:

1. Place the ham at room temperature for about 30 minutes before cooking.
2. In a bowl, mix together the whiskey, mustard, and honey.
3. Place the ham in a baking dish that fits in the air fryer.
4. Top with half of the honey mixture and coat well.
5. Set the temperature of Air Fryer to 160 degrees C and preheat for 5 minutes.
6. After preheating, arrange the baking dish into the air fryer basket.
7. Slide the basket in Air Fryer and set the time for 40 minutes.
8. After 15 minutes of cooking, flip the side of ham and top with the remaining honey mixture.
9. Remove from air fryer and place the ham onto a platter for about 10 minutes before slicing. C
10. Cut the ham into desired size slices and serve.

Herbed Leg of Lamb

Servings|5 Time|1 hour 25 minutes

Nutritional Content (per serving):

Cal| 468   Fat| 36.2g   Protein| 32.2g   Carbs| 0.7g

Ingredients:

- 907 grams bone-in leg of lamb
- Salt and ground black pepper, as required
- 2 fresh thyme sprigs
- 30 milliliters olive oil
- 2 fresh rosemary sprigs

Directions:

1. Coat the leg of lamb with oil and sprinkle with salt and black pepper.
2. Wrap the leg of lamb with herb sprigs.
3. Set the temperature of Air Fryer to 150 degrees C and preheat for 5 minutes.
4. After preheating, arrange the leg of lamb into the greased air fryer basket.
5. Slide the basket in Air Fryer and set the time for 75 minutes.
6. Remove from Air Fryer and transfer the leg of lamb onto a platter.
7. With a piece of foil, cover the leg of lamb for about 10 minutes before slicing.
8. Cut the leg of lamb into desired size pieces and serve.

Leg of Lamb with Brussels Sprout

Servings|6   Time|2 hours

Nutritional Content (per serving):

Cal| 41   Fat| 18.9g   Protein| 47.3g   Carbs| 15.8g

Ingredients:

- 925 grams leg of lamb
- 2 grams fresh rosemary, minced
- 1 garlic clove, minced
- 680 grams Brussels sprouts, trimmed
- 45 milliliters olive oil, divided
- 2 grams fresh lemon thyme
- Salt and ground black pepper, as required
- 35 grams honey

Directions:

1. With a sharp knife, score the leg of lamb at several places.
2. In a bowl, mix together 30 milliliters of oil, herbs, garlic, salt, and black pepper.
3. Generously coat the leg of lamb with oil mixture.
4. Set the temperature of Air Fryer to 150 degrees C and preheat for 5 minutes.
5. After preheating, arrange the leg of lamb into the greased Air Fryer basket.
6. Slide the basket in Air Fryer and set the time for 75 minutes.
7. Meanwhile, coat the Brussels sprout evenly with the remaining oil and honey.
8. After 75 minutes of cooking, set the temperature of Air Fryer to 200 degrees C.
9. Place the leg of lamb onto a platter and with a piece of foil, cover for about 10 minutes before slicing.
10. Cut the leg of lamb into desired size pieces and serve alongside the Brussels sprout.

Spiced Lamb Steaks

Servings|3   Time|30 minutes

Nutritional Content (per serving):

Cal| 368   Fat| 17.9g   Protein| 48.9g   Carbs| 4.2g

Ingredients:

- ❖ ½ of onion, roughly chopped
- ❖ 5 grams ground fennel
- ❖ 2½ grams ground cinnamon
- ❖ Salt and ground black pepper, as required
- ❖ 5 garlic cloves, peeled
- ❖ 3 grams fresh ginger, peeled
- ❖ 2½ grams ground cumin
- ❖ 2½ grams cayenne pepper
- ❖ 681 grams boneless lamb sirloin steaks

Directions:

1. In a blender, add the onion, garlic, ginger, and spices and pulse until smooth.
2. Transfer the mixture into a large bowl.
3. Add the lamb steaks and coat with the mixture generously.
4. Refrigerate to marinate for about 24 hours.
5. Set the temperature of Air Fryer to 165 degrees C and preheat for 5 minutes.
6. After preheating, arrange the steaks into the greased air fryer basket in a single layer.
7. Slide the basket in Air Fryer and set the time for 15 minutes.
8. Flip the steaks once halfway through.
9. Serve hot.

Pesto Rack of Lamb

Servings|4   Time|31 minutes

Nutritional Content (per serving):

Cal| 406   Fat| 27.7g   Protein| 34.9g   Carbs| 2.9g

Ingredients:

- ❖ ½ bunch fresh mint
- ❖ 60 milliliters extra-virgin olive oil
- ❖ Salt and ground black pepper, as required
- ❖ 1 garlic clove, peeled
- ❖ 10 grams honey
- ❖ 1 (680-gramss) rack of lamb

Directions:

1. For pesto: in a blender, add the mint, garlic, oil, honey, salt, and black pepper and pulse until smooth.
2. Coat the rack of lamb with pesto evenly.
3. Set the temperature of Air Fryer to 95 degrees C and preheat for 5 minutes.
4. After preheating, place the rack of lamb into the prepared Air Fryer basket.
5. Slide the basket into the Air Fryer and set the time for 15 minutes.
6. While cooking, coat the rack of lamb with the remaining pesto after every 5 minutes.
7. Remove from Air Fryer and place the rack of lamb onto a cutting board for about 5 minutes.
8. Cut the rack into individual chops and serve.

Herbed Lamb Chops

Servings|2   Time|17 minutes

Nutritional Content (per serving):

Cal| 251   Fat| 12.3g   Protein| 32.5g   Carbs| 1.1g

Ingredients:

- 15 milliliters fresh lemon juice
- 1½ grams dried rosemary
- 2½ grams ground cumin
- Salt and ground black pepper, as required
- 15 milliliters olive oil
- 1½ grams dried thyme
- 2½ grams ground coriander
- 4 (115-gram) lamb chops

Directions:

1. In a bowl, mix together the lemon juice, oil, herbs, and spices.
2. Add the chops and coat with the herb mixture evenly.
3. Refrigerate to marinate for about 1 hour.
4. Set the temperature of Air Fryer to 200 degrees C and preheat for 5 minutes.
5. After preheating, arrange the chops into the greased Air Fryer basket.
6. Slide the basket in Air Fryer and set the time for 7 minutes.
7. Flip the chops once halfway through.
8. Serve hot.

Fish & Seafood Recipes

Simple Salmon

Servings|2   Time|15 minutes

Nutritional Content (per serving):

Cal| 286   Fat| 17.6g   Protein| 33g   Carbs| 0g

Ingredients:

- ❖ 2 (170-gram) salmon fillets
- ❖ 15 milliliters olive oil
- ❖ Salt and ground black pepper, as required

Directions:

1. Season each salmon fillet with salt and black pepper and then, coat with the oil.
2. Set the temperature of Air Fryer to 185 degrees C and preheat for 5 minutes.
3. After preheating, arrange the salmon fillets into Air Fryer basket.
4. Slide the basket in Air Fryer and set the time for 10 minutes.
5. Serve hot.

Spicy Salmon

Servings|2   Time|21 minutes

Nutritional Content (per serving):

Cal| 277   Fat| 15.4g   Protein| 33.5g   Carbs| 2.5g

Ingredients:

- ❖ 5 grams smoked paprika
- ❖ 5 grams onion powder
- ❖ Salt and ground black pepper, as required
- ❖ 10 milliliters olive oil
- ❖ 5 grams garlic powder
- ❖ 2 (150-grams) (3¾-centimeters thick) salmon fillets
- ❖ 5 grams cayenne pepper

Directions:

1. In a bowl, add the spices and mix well.
2. Drizzle the salmon fillets with oil and then, rub with the spice mixture.
3. Set the temperature of Air Fryer to 200 degrees C and preheat for 5 minutes.
4. After preheating, arrange the salmon fillets into the greased air fryer basket.
5. Slide the basket in Air Fryer and set the time for 11 minutes.
6. Serve hot.

Maple Salmon

Servings|2   Time|18 minutes

Nutritional Content (per serving):

Cal| 277   Fat| 10.5g   Protein| 33g   Carbs| 13.4g

Ingredients:

- ❖ 2 (150-grams) salmon fillets
- ❖ 35 grams maple syrup
- ❖ Salt, as required

Directions:

1. Sprinkle the salmon fillets with salt and then, coat with maple syrup.
2. Set the temperature of Air Fryer to 180 degrees C and preheat for 5 minutes.
3. After preheating, arrange the salmon fillets into the greased air fryer basket.
4. Slide the basket in Air Fryer and set the time for 8 minutes.
5. Serve hot.

Salmon with Asparagus

Servings|2   Time|21 minutes

Nutritional Content (per serving):

Cal| 314   Fat| 17.9g   Protein| 35.8g   Carbs| 5.2g

Ingredients:

- ❖ 2 (170-gram) boneless salmon fillets
- ❖ 2 grams fresh parsley, chopped
- ❖ 225 grams asparagus

- ❖ 15 milliliters olive oil
- ❖ 2 grams fresh dill, chopped
- ❖ Salt and ground black pepper, as required

- ❖ 20 milliliters fresh lemon juice

Directions:

1. In a small bowl, mix together the lemon juice, oil, herbs, salt, and black pepper.
2. In a large bowl, mix together the salmon and ¾ of oil mixture.
3. In a second large bowl, add the asparagus and remaining oil mixture and mix well.
4. Set the temperature of Air Fryer to 205 degrees C and preheat for 5 minutes.
5. After preheating, arrange the salmon fillets into the greased Air Fryer basket.
6. Slide the basket in Air Fryer and set the time for 11 minutes.
7. After 3 minutes of cooking, arrange the salmon fillets on top of asparagus.
8. Serve the salmon fillets alongside the asparagus.

Crispy Cod

Servings|4   Time|30 minutes

Nutritional Content (per serving):

Cal| 204   Fat| 4.7g   Protein| 24.6g   Carbs| 6.9g

Ingredients:

- ❖ 4 (115-gram) cod fillets
- ❖ 15 grams all-purpose flour
- ❖ 60 grams panko breadcrumbs
- ❖ 2½ grams dry mustard
- ❖ 2½ grams onion powder
- ❖ Olive oil cooking spray
- ❖ Salt, as required
- ❖ 2 eggs
- ❖ 2 grams fresh dill, minced
- ❖ 2½ grams lemon zest, grated
- ❖ 2½ grams paprika

Directions:

1. Season the cod fillets with salt generously.
2. In a shallow bowl, place the flour.
3. Crack the eggs in a second bowl and beat well.
4. In a third bowl, mix together the panko, dill, lemon zest, mustard and spices.
5. Coat each cod fillet with the flour, then dip into beaten eggs and finally, coat with panko mixture.
6. Set the temperature of Air Fryer to 205 degrees C and preheat for 5 minutes.
7. After preheating, arrange the cod fillets into the greased Air Fryer basket.
8. Spray the tops of fillets with cooking spray.
9. Slide the basket in Air Fryer and set the time for 15 minutes.
10. Flip the cod fillets once hallway through.
11. Serve hot.

Ranch Tilapia

Servings|4   Time|23 minutes

Nutritional Content (per serving):

Cal| 274   Fat| 14.4g   Protein| 31.1g   Carbs| 4.9g

Ingredients:

- ❖ 21 grams cornflakes, crushed
- ❖ 25 milliliters vegetable oil
- ❖ 2 eggs
- ❖ 1 (28-grams) packet dry ranch-style dressing mix
- ❖ 4 (150-grams) tilapia fillets

Directions:

1. In a shallow bowl, beat the eggs. In another bowl, add the cornflakes, ranch dressing, and oil and mix until a crumbly mixture forms.
2. Dip the fish fillets into egg and then coat with the cornflake mixture.
3. Set the temperature of Air Fryer to 180 degrees C and preheat for 5 minutes.
4. After preheating, arrange the tilapia fillets into the greased air fryer basket.
5. Slide the basket in Air Fryer and set the time for 13 minutes.
6. Serve hot.

Breaded Flounder

Servings|4   Time|22minutes

Nutritional Content (per serving):

Cal| 456   Fat| 20.2g   Protein| 40.2g   Carbs| 5.4g

Ingredients:

- ❖ 1 egg
- ❖ 60 milliliters vegetable oil
- ❖ 1 lemon, sliced
- ❖ 120 grams dry breadcrumbs
- ❖ 4 (170-gram) flounder fillets

Directions:

1. In a shallow bowl, beat the egg
2. In another bowl, add the breadcrumbs and oil. Mix until crumbly mixture is formed.
3. Dip flounder fillets into the beaten egg and then, coat with the breadcrumb mixture.
4. Set the temperature of Air Fryer to 180 degrees C and preheat for 5 minutes.
5. After preheating, arrange the flounder fillets into the greased Air Fryer basket in a single layer.
6. Slide the basket in Air Fryer and set the time for 12 minutes.
7. Serve hot with the garnishing of lemon slices.

Glazed Halibut

Servings|3   Time|30 minutes

Nutritional Content (per serving):

Cal| 291   Fat| 3.6g   Protein| 34.9g   Carbs| 17.3g

Ingredients:

- ❖ 1 garlic clove, minced
- ❖ 120 milliliters cooking wine
- ❖ 60 milliliters fresh orange juice
- ❖ 50 grams sugar
- ❖ 455 grams halibut steak

- ❖ 120 milliliters low-sodium soy sauce

- ❖ 30 milliliters fresh lime juice
- ❖ 1¼ grams red pepper flakes, crushed
- ❖ 1 gram fresh ginger, grated

Directions:

1. In a medium pan, add garlic, ginger, wine, soy sauce, juices, sugar, and red pepper flakes and bring to a boil.
2. Cook for about 3-4 minutes, stirring continuously.
3. Remove the pan of the marinade from heat and let it cool.
4. In a small bowl, add half of the marinade and reserve in a refrigerator.
5. In a resealable bag, add the remaining marinade and halibut steak.
6. Seal the bag and shake to coat well. Refrigerate for about 30 minutes.
7. Set the temperature of Air Fryer to 200 degrees C and preheat for 5 minutes.
8. After preheating, arrange the halibut steak into the air fryer basket.
9. Slide the basket in Air Fryer and set the time for 11 minutes.
10. Remove from air fryer and place the halibut steak onto a platter.
11. Cut the steak into 3 equal-sized pieces and coat with the remaining glaze.
12. Serve immediately.

Cajun Catfish

Servings|2   Time|24 minutes

Nutritional Content (per serving):

Cal| 335   Fat| 20.3g   Protein| 27.7g   Carbs| 9.6g

Ingredients:

- ❖ 20 grams cornmeal polenta
- ❖ 2½ grams paprika
- ❖ Salt, as required
- ❖ 15 milliliters olive oil

- ❖ 10 grams Cajun seasoning
- ❖ 2½ grams garlic powder
- ❖ 2 (170-gram) catfish fillets

Directions:

1. In a bowl, mix together the cornmeal, Cajun seasoning, paprika, garlic powder, and salt.
2. Add the catfish fillets and coat evenly with the mixture.
3. Now, coat each fillet with oil.
4. Set the temperature of Air Fryer to 205 degrees C and preheat for 5 minutes.
5. After preheating, arrange the catfish fillets into the greased Air Fryer basket in a single layer.
6. Slide the basket in Air Fryer and set the time for 13-14 minutes.
7. Flip the catfish fillets once halfway through.
8. Serve hot.

Sesame Seed Tuna

Servings|2   Time|16 minutes

Nutritional Content (per serving):

Cal| 399   Fat| 19.4g   Protein| 50.2g   Carbs| 4.8g

Ingredients:

- ❖ 1 egg white
- ❖ 8 grams black sesame seeds
- ❖ 2 (150-grams) tuna steaks
- ❖ 30 grams white sesame seeds
- ❖ Salt and ground black pepper, as required

Directions:

1. In a shallow bowl, beat the egg white.
2. In another bowl, mix together the sesame seeds, salt, and black pepper.
3. Dip the tuna steaks into egg white and then coat with the sesame seeds mixture.
4. Set the temperature of Air Fryer to 205 degrees C and preheat for 5 minutes.
5. After preheating, arrange the tuna steaks into the greased air fryer basket.
6. Slide the basket in Air Fryer and set the time for 6 minutes.
7. Flip the tuna steaks once halfway through.
8. Serve hot.

Spicy Shrimp

Servings|2   Time|20 minutes

Nutritional Content (per serving):

Cal| 253   Fat| 11.5g   Protein| 35.7g   Carbs| 0.7g

Ingredients:

- ❖ 340 grams tiger shrimp, peeled and deveined
- ❖ 1¼ grams smoked paprika
- ❖ Salt, as required
- ❖ 20 milliliters olive oil
- ❖ 2½ grams old bay seasoning
- ❖ 1¼ grams cayenne pepper

Directions:

1. Set the temperature of Air Fryer to 200 degrees C and preheat for 5 minutes.
2. In a large bowl, mix well shrimp, oil, and spices.
3. After preheating, arrange the shrimp into the greased Air Fryer basket in a single layer.
4. Slide the basket in Air Fryer and set the time for 5 minutes.
5. Serve hot.

Shrimp Scampi

Servings|4   Time|23 minutes

Nutritional Content (per serving):

Cal| 781   Fat| 13.7g   Protein| 81g   Carbs| 3.3g

Ingredients:

- 40 grams salted butter
- 4 grams garlic, minced
- 455 grams shrimp, peeled and deveined
- 2 grams fresh chives, chopped
- 15 grams fresh lemon juice
- 10 grams red pepper flakes, crushed
- 3 grams fresh basil, chopped
- 15 milliliters dry white wine

Directions:

1. Arrange a 17½-centimeters round baking pan into the air fryer basket.
2. Slide the basket in Air Fryer and set the temperature of Air Fryer to 160 degrees C.
3. Preheat for 5 minutes.
4. After preheating, carefully remove the hot pan from air fryer basket.
5. In the heated pan, place butter, lemon juice, garlic, and red pepper flakes and return the pan to Air fryer basket.
6. Set the time for 2 minutes.
7. With a wooden spoon, stir the mixture once halfway through.
8. Carefully remove the pan from Air fryer basket and stir in shrimp, basil, chives and wine.
9. Return the pan to air fryer basket and set the time for 5 minutes.
10. With a wooden spoon, stir the mixture once halfway through.
11. Place the pan onto a wire rack for about 1 minute.
12. Stir the mixture and transfer onto serving plates.
13. Serve hot.

Shrimp Kabobs

Servings|2   Time|23 minutes

Nutritional Content (per serving):

Cal| 212   Fat| 3.2g   Protein| 39.1g   Carbs| 3.9g

Ingredients:

- ❖ 340 grams shrimp, peeled and deveined
- ❖ 2 grams garlic, minced
- ❖ 2½ grams ground cumin
- ❖ Salt and ground black pepper, as required
- ❖ 30 milliliters fresh lemon juice
- ❖ 2½ grams paprika
- ❖ 2½ grams ground cumin
- ❖ 2 grams fresh Coriander, chopped

Directions:

1. In a bowl, mix together the lemon juice, garlic, and spices.
2. Add the shrimp and mix well.
3. Thread the shrimp onto presoaked wooden skewers.
4. Set the temperature of Air Fryer to 175 degrees C and preheat for 5 minutes.
5. After preheating, arrange the shrimp skewers into the air fryer basket.
6. Slide the basket in Air Fryer and set the time for 8 minutes.
7. Flip the skewers once halfway through.
8. Transfer the shrimp kebabs onto serving plates.
9. Garnish with fresh Coriander and serve immediately.

Buttered Scallops

Servings|2   Time|14 minutes

Nutritional Content (per serving):

Cal| 206   Fat| 7.4g   Protein| 28,7g   Carbs| 4.7g

Ingredients:

- ❖ 340 grams sea scallops, cleaned and patted very dry
- ❖ Salt and ground black pepper, as required
- ❖ 15 grams butter, melted
- ❖ 2 grams fresh thyme, minced

Directions:

1. In a large bowl, add the scallops, butter, thyme, salt, and black pepper. Toss to coat well.
2. Set the temperature of Air Fryer to 200 degrees C and preheat for 5 minutes.
3. Arrange scallops into the greased Air Fryer basket in a single layer.
4. Slide the basket in Air Fryer and set the time for 4 minutes.
5. Serve hot.

Scallops with Spinach

Servings|2   Time|25 minutes

Nutritional Content (per serving):

Cal| 203   Fat| 18.3g   Protein| 26.4g   Carbs| 12.3g

Ingredients:

- 1 (340-grams) package frozen spinach, thawed and drained
- Salt and ground black pepper, as required
- 20 grams tomato paste
- 2 grams garlic, minced
- 2 grams fresh basil, chopped
- 8 jumbo sea scallops
- Olive oil cooking spray
- 210 grams heavy whipping cream

Directions:

1. In the bottom of a 17½ centimeters heatproof pan, place the spinach.
2. Spray with cooking spray and then sprinkle with a little salt and black pepper.
3. Arrange scallops on top of the spinach in a single layer.
4. In a bowl, mix well cream, tomato paste, garlic, basil, salt, and black pepper.
5. Place the cream mixture evenly over the spinach and scallops.
6. Set the temperature of Air Fryer to 175 degrees C and preheat for 5 minutes.
7. After preheating, arrange the pan into the air fryer basket.
8. Slide the basket in Air Fryer and set the time for 10 minutes.
9. Serve hot.

Vegetarian Recipes

Jacket Potatoes

Servings|2   Time|25 minutes

Nutritional Content (per serving):

Cal| 253   Fat| 11.3g   Protein| 4.8g   Carbs| 34.5g

Ingredients:

- ❖ 2 potatoes
- ❖ 45 grams sour cream
- ❖ 15 grams butter, softened
- ❖ 2 grams fresh chives, minced
- ❖ 10 grams mozzarella cheese, shredded
- ❖ Salt and ground black pepper, as required

Directions:

1. With a fork, prick the potatoes.
2. Set the temperature of Air Fryer to 180 degrees C and preheat for 5 minutes.
3. After preheating, arrange the potatoes into the greased Air Fryer basket.
4. Slide the basket in Air Fryer and set the time for 15 minutes.
5. Meanwhile, in a bowl, add the remaining Ingredients: and mix until well combined.
6. Transfer the potatoes onto a platter.
7. Open potatoes from the center and stuff them with cheese mixture.
8. Serve immediately.

Feta Spinach

Servings|6   Time|21 minutes

Nutritional Content (per serving):

Cal| 153   Fat| 12.2g   Protein| 7.1g   Carbs| 6.7g

Ingredients:

- ❖ 910 grams fresh spinach, chopped
- ❖ 1 jalapeño pepper, minced
- ❖ Salt and ground black pepper, as required
- ❖ 5 grams fresh lemon zest, grated
- ❖ 1 garlic clove, minced
- ❖ 40 grams butter, melted
- ❖ 110 grams feta cheese, crumbled

Directions:

1. In a bowl, add the spinach, garlic, jalapeño, butter, salt and black pepper and mix well.
2. Set the temperature of Air Fryer to 170 degrees C and preheat for 5 minutes.
3. After preheating, arrange the spinach mixture into the greased air fryer basket.
4. Slide the basket in Air Fryer and set the time for 15 minutes.
5. Remove from the air Fryer and transfer the spinach mixture into a bowl.
6. Immediately stir in the cheese and lemon zest and serve hot.

Goat Cheese Kale

Servings|4   Time|25 minutes

Nutritional Content (per serving):

Cal| 272   Fat| 20.5g   Protein| 11.8g   Carbs| 12.5g

Ingredients:

- 455 grams fresh kale, tough ribs removed and chopped
- 110 grams goat cheese, crumbled
- 5 milliliters fresh lemon juice
- 45 milliliters olive oil
- Salt and ground black pepper, as required

Directions:

1. In a bowl, add the kale, oil, salt and black pepper and mix well.
2. Set the temperature of Air Fryer to 170 degrees C and preheat for 5 minutes.
3. After preheating, arrange the kale into Air Fryer basket.
4. Slide the basket in Air Fryer and set the time for 15 minutes.
5. Transfer the kale mixture into a bowl.
6. Immediately stir in the cheese and lemon juice.
7. Serve hot.

Parmesan Brussels Sprout

Servings|3   Time|20 minutes

Nutritional Content (per serving):

Cal| 169   Fat| 7.6g   Protein| 9.7g   Carbs| 20.2g

Ingredients:

- ❖ 455 grams Brussels sprouts, trimmed and halved
- ❖ Salt and ground black pepper, as required
- ❖ 27½ grams Parmesan cheese, shredded
- ❖ 15 milliliters balsamic vinegar
- ❖ 15 milliliters extra-virgin olive oil
- ❖ 25 grams whole-wheat breadcrumbs

Directions:

1. Set the temperature of Air Fryer to 205 degrees C and preheat for 5 minutes.
2. In a bowl, mix together the Brussels sprouts, vinegar, oil, salt, and black pepper.
3. After preheating, arrange Brussels sprouts into the greased air fryer basket in a single layer.
4. Slide the basket in Air Fryer and set the time for 5 minutes.
5. Remove from Air Fryer and flip the Brussels sprouts.
6. Sprinkle the Brussels sprouts with breadcrumbs, followed by the cheese.
7. Slide the basket in Air Fryer and set the time for 5 minutes.
8. Serve hot.

Spiced Sweet Potato

Servings|4   Time|30 minutes

Nutritional Content (per serving):

Cal| 198   Fat| 7.3g   Protein| 1.9g   Carbs| 32g

Ingredients:

- ❖ 3 large sweet potatoes, peeled and cut in 1-inch cubes
- ❖ 2½ grams ground cumin
- ❖ 2½ grams red chili powder
- ❖ 30 milliliters vegetable oil
- ❖ Pinch of dried parsley
- ❖ Salt and ground black pepper, as required

Directions:

1. In a large bowl, add all the Ingredients: and toss to coat well.
2. Set the temperature of Air Fryer to 210 degrees C and preheat for 5 minutes.
3. After preheating, arrange the sweet potato cubes into the greased Air Fryer basket in a single layer.
4. Slide the basket in Air Fryer and set the time for 20 minutes.
5. Serve hot.

Caramelized Carrots

Servings|3   Time|25 minutes

Nutritional Content (per serving):

Cal| 416   Fat| 20g   Protein| 1.3g   Carbs| 36.2g

Ingredients:

- ❖ 115 grams butter, melted
- ❖ 1 small bag baby carrots

- ❖ 100 grams brown sugar

Directions:

1. Set the temperature of Air Fryer to 205 degrees C and preheat for 5 minutes.
2. In a bowl, mix together the butter and brown sugar.
3. Add the carrots and coat well.
4. After preheating, arrange carrots into the greased Air Fryer basket in a single layer.
5. Slide the basket in Air Fryer and set the time for 15 minutes.
6. Serve hot.

Wine Braised Mushrooms

Servings|6   Time|42 minutes

Nutritional Content (per serving):

Cal| 56   Fat| 2.5g   Protein| 4.8g   Carbs| 5.4g

Ingredients:

- ❖ 15 grams butter
- ❖ 2 pounds fresh mushrooms, quartered
- ❖ 10 grams Herbs de Provence
- ❖ 2½ grams garlic powder
- ❖ 30 milliliters white wine

Directions:

1. Set the temperature of air fryer to 320 degrees F.
2. In the air fryer pan, mix together the butter, Herbs de Provence, and garlic powder.
3. Slide the pan in Air Fryer and set the time for 31 minutes.
4. After 2 minutes of cooking, stir in the mushrooms.
5. After 27 minutes of cooking, stir in the wine.
6. Serve hot.

Vinegar Broccoli

Servings|2   Time|50 minutes

Nutritional Content (per serving):

Cal| 140   Fat| 9.3g   Protein| 6.5g   Carbs| 10.3g

Ingredients:

- 285 grams frozen broccoli
- 15 milliliters olive oil
- Salt and ground black pepper, as required
- 45 milliliters balsamic vinegar
- 1¼ grams cayenne pepper
- 15 grams Parmesan cheese, grated

Directions:

1. In a bowl, add the broccoli, vinegar, oil, cayenne, salt, and black pepper and toss to coat well.
2. Set the temperature of Air Fryer to 205 degrees C and preheat for 5 minutes.
3. After preheating, arrange broccoli into the greased Air Fryer basket.
4. Slide the basket in Air Fryer and set the time for 20 minutes.
5. While cooking, toss the broccoli occasionally.
6. Serve hot.

Mushrooms with Peas

Servings|4   Time|25 minutes

Nutritional Content (per serving):

Cal| 129   Fat| 0.2g   Protein| 6g   Carbs| 24.3g

Ingredients:

- ❖ 120 milliliters soy sauce
- ❖ 60 milliliters rice vinegar
- ❖ 10 grams Chinese five-spice powder
- ❖ 450 grams Cremini mushrooms, halved

- ❖ 55 grams maple syrup
- ❖ 4 garlic cloves, finely chopped
- ❖ 2½ grams ground ginger
- ❖ 73 grams frozen peas

Directions:

1. In a bowl, add the soy sauce, maple syrup, vinegar, garlic, five-spice powder, and ground ginger and mix well.
2. Set the temperature of Air Fryer to 175 degrees C and preheat for 5 minutes.
3. After preheating, arrange the mushroom into the greased air fryer pan.
4. Slide the pan in Air Fryer and set the time for 15 minutes.
5. After 10 minutes of cooking, in the pan, add the peas and vinegar mixture and stir to combine.
6. Serve hot.

Veggie Casserole

Servings|6   Time|27 minutes

Nutritional Content (per serving):

Cal| 184   Fat| 12.2g   Protein| 3.6g   Carbs| 15.9g

Ingredients:

- ❖ 680 grams fresh green beans, trimmed
- ❖ 45 milliliters olive oil
- ❖ 5 grams ground sage
- ❖ 5 grams onion powder
- ❖ 220 grams fresh button mushrooms, sliced
- ❖ 60 milliliters fresh lemon juice
- ❖ 5 grams garlic powder
- ❖ 65 grams French fried onions

Directions:

1. In a bowl, add the green beans, mushrooms, oil, lemon juice, sage, and spices and toss to coat well.
2. Set the temperature of Air Fryer to 205 degrees C and preheat for 5 minutes.
3. After preheating, arrange mushroom mixture into the greased Air Fryer basket.
4. Slide the basket in Air Fryer and set the time for 10-12 minutes
5. Shake the basket several times while cooking.
6. Transfer the mushroom mixture into a serving dish.
7. Top with fried onions and serve.

Stuffed Tomatoes

Servings|4   Time|37 minutes

Nutritional Content (per serving):

Cal| 421   Fat| 2.2g   Protein| 10.5g   Carbs| 89.1g

Ingredients:

- ❖ 4 tomatoes
- ❖ 1 carrot, peeled and finely chopped
- ❖ 145 grams frozen peas, thawed
- ❖ 500 grams cold cooked rice
- ❖ 5 grams olive oil
- ❖ 1 onion, chopped
- ❖ 1 garlic clove, minced
- ❖ 15 milliliters soy sauce

Directions:

1. Cut the top of each tomato and scoop out pulp and seeds.
2. In a skillet, heat oil over low heat and sauté the carrot, onion, garlic, and peas for about 2 minutes.
3. Stir in the soy sauce and rice and remove from heat.
4. Stuff each tomato with the rice mixture.
5. Set the temperature of Air Fryer to 180 degrees C and preheat for 5 minutes.
6. After preheating, arrange the tomatoes into the greased air fryer basket.
7. Slide the basket in Air Fryer and set the time for 20 minutes.
8. Remove from air fryer and transfer the tomatoes onto a serving platter.
9. Set aside to cool slightly.
10. Serve warm.

Oats & Beans Stuffed Capsicum

Servings|2   Time|31 minutes

Nutritional Content (per serving):

Cal| 453   Fat| 19.1g   Protein| 7.4g   Carbs| 81g

Ingredients:

- ❖ 2 large capsicums, halved lengthwise and seeded
- ❖ 70 grams coconut yogurt
- ❖ Salt and ground black pepper, as required
- ❖ 468 grams cooked oatmeal
- ❖ 55 grams canned red kidney beans, rinsed and drained
- ❖ 1¼ grams smoked paprika
- ❖ 1¼ grams ground cumin

Directions:

1. Set the temperature of Air Fryer to 180 degrees C and preheat for 5 minutes.
2. After preheating, arrange the capsicums into the greased air fryer basket, cut-side down.
3. Slide the basket in Air Fryer and set the time for 8 minutes.
4. Remove from the air fryer and set the capsicums aside to cool.
5. Meanwhile, in a bowl, add the oatmeal, beans, coconut yogurt, and spices and mix well.
6. Stuff each capsicum half with the oatmeal mixture.
7. Now, set the Air Fryer to 180 degrees C.
8. Arrange capsicums into the air fryer basket.
9. Slide the basket in Air Fryer and set the time for 8 minutes.
10. Remove from air fryer and transfer the capsicums onto a serving platter.
11. Serve warm.

Tofu with Cauliflower

Servings|2   Time|30 minutes

Nutritional Content (per serving):

Cal| 170   Fat| 11.9g   Protein| 11.6g   Carbs| 8.3g

Ingredients:

- 1½ (1113-grams) block firm tofu, pressed and cubed
- 10 grams nutritional yeast
- 5 grams ground turmeric
- Salt and ground black pepper, as required
- ½ of small head cauliflower, cut into florets
- 15 milliliters canola oil
- 1¼ grams dried parsley
- 1¼ grams paprika

Directions:

1. In a bowl, add all the ingredients and mix well.
2. Set the temperature of Air Fryer to 200 degrees C and preheat for 5 minutes.
3. After preheating, arrange the tofu mixture into the greased air fryer basket.
4. Slide the basket in Air Fryer and set the time for 15 minutes.
5. Shake the basket once halfway through.
6. Serve hot.

Beans & Veggies Burgers

Servings|4   Time|42 minutes

Nutritional Content (per serving):

Cal| 121   Fat| 0.4g   Protein| 26.2g   Carbs| 24.3g

Ingredients:

- ❖ 172 grams cooked black bean
- ❖ 30 grams fresh spinach, chopped
- ❖ 10 grams Chile lime seasoning
- ❖ 330 grams boiled potatoes, peeled and mashed
- ❖ 100 grams fresh mushrooms, chopped
- ❖ Olive oil cooking spray

Directions:

1. In a large bowl, add the beans, potatoes, spinach, mushrooms, and seasoning and with your hands, mix until well combined.
2. Make 4 equal-sized patties from the mixture.
3. Set the temperature of Air Fryer to 190 degrees C and preheat for 5 minutes.
4. After preheating, arrange the patties into the greased air fryer basket.
5. Slide the basket in Air Fryer and set the time for 19 minutes.
6. After 12 minutes of cooking, flip the patties.
7. After 19 minutes of cooking, set the temperature of Air Fryer to 32 degrees C for 3 more minutes.
8. Serve warm.

Veggie Rice

Servings|3   Time|33 minutes

Nutritional Content (per serving):

Cal| 350   Fat| 10g   Protein| 8.1g   Carbs| 54.7g

Ingredients:

- ❖ 500 grams cooked white rice
- ❖ 10 milliliters sesame oil, toasted and divided
- ❖ Salt and ground white pepper, as required
- ❖ 73 grams frozen peas, thawed
- ❖ 5 milliliters low-sodium soy sauce
- ❖ 3 grams sesame seeds, toasted
- ❖ 1 5 milliliters vegetable oil
- ❖ 15 milliliters water
- ❖ 1 large egg, lightly beaten
- ❖ 45 grams frozen carrots, thawed
- ❖ 5 milliliters Sriracha sauce

Directions:

1. In a large bowl, add the rice, vegetable oil, 5 milliliters of sesame oil, water, salt, and white pepper and mix well.
2. Set the temperature of Air Fryer to 195 degrees C and preheat for 5 minutes.
3. After preheating, place the rice mixture into the greased air fryer pan.
4. Slide the pan in Air Fryer and set the time for 18 minutes.
5. After 6 minutes of cooking, stir the rice mixture.
6. After 12 minutes of cooking, place the beaten egg over rice mixture.
7. After 16 minutes of cooking, stir in the peas and carrots.
8. Meanwhile, in a bowl, mix together soy sauce, Sriracha sauce, sesame seeds and the remaining sesame oil.
9. Remove from Air Fryer and transfer the rice mixture into a serving bowl.
10. Drizzle with the sauce and serve.

Snacks Recipes

Roasted Cashews

Servings|8   Time|14 minutes

Nutritional Content (per serving):

Cal| 201   Fat| 10g   Protein| 16.4g   Carbs| 11.2g

Ingredients:

- ❖ 260 grams raw cashews
- ❖ Salt and ground black pepper, as required
- ❖ 5 grams butter, melted

Directions:

1. In a bowl, mix together all the ingredients.
2. Set the temperature of Air Fryer to 180 degrees C and preheat for 5 minutes.
3. After preheating, arrange the cashews into the greased air fryer basket in a single layer.
4. Slide the basket in Air Fryer and set the time for 4 minutes.
5. Shake the cashews once halfway through.
6. transfer the hot nuts in a glass bowl and set aside to cool completely before serving.

Roasted Peanuts

Servings|4   Time|19 minutes

Nutritional Content (per serving):

Cal| 214   Fat| 18.6g   Protein| 9.7g   Carbs| 6.1g

Ingredients:

- ❖ 150 grams raw peanuts
- ❖ Salt, as required
- ❖ 10 milliliters olive oil

Directions:

1. Set the temperature of Air Fryer to 180 degrees C and preheat for 5 minutes.
2. After preheating, arrange the peanuts into the greased Air fryer basket.
3. Slide the basket in Air Fryer and set the time for 15 minutes.
4. After 9 minutes of cooking, transfer the peanuts into a large bowl.
5. Add the oil and salt and toss to coat well.
6. Return the peanuts into the Air Fryer basket and insert into the Air Fryer.
7. Transfer the peanuts into a large bowl and set aside to cool completely before serving.

French Fries

Servings|8   Time|45 minutes

Nutritional Content (per serving):

Cal| 132   Fat| 7.3g   Protein| 1.8g   Carbs| 16.2g

Ingredients:

- ❖ 795 grams potatoes, peeled and cut into strips
- ❖ 5 grams onion powder
- ❖ 60 milliliters olive oil
- ❖ 10 grams paprika

Directions:

1. In a large bowl, add the water and potato strips.
2. Set aside for about 1 hour.
3. Drain the potato strips well and pat them dry with paper towels.
4. In a large bowl, add the potato strips and the remaining ingredients and toss to coat well.
5. Set the temperature of Air Fryer to 190 degrees C and preheat for 5 minutes.
6. After preheating, arrange the potato strips into the air fryer basket in a single layer.
7. Slide the basket in Air Fryer and set the time for 30 minutes.
8. Serve warm.

Carrot Sticks

Servings|2   Time|22 minutes

Nutritional Content (per serving):

Cal| 118   Fat| 7.4g   Protein| 0.4g   Carbs| 14.5g

Ingredients:

- ❖ 1 carrot, peeled and cut into sticks
- ❖ 15 milliliters olive oil
- ❖ 1¼ grams cayenne pepper
- ❖ 20 grams sugar
- ❖ Salt and ground black pepper, as required

- ❖ 2 grams fresh rosemary, finely chopped

Directions:

1. In a bowl, add all the Ingredients: and toss to coat well.
2. Set the temperature of Air Fryer to 200 degrees C and preheat for 5 minutes.
3. After preheating, arrange the carrot sticks in the Air Fryer basket in a single layer.
4. Slide the basket in Air Fryer and set the time for 12 minutes.
5. Serve hot.

Onion Rings

Servings|4   Time|30 minutes

Nutritional Content (per serving):

Cal| 285   Fat| 3.8g   Protein| 10.5g   Carbs| 51.6g

Ingredients:

- 1 large onion, cut into 0.60-centimeters slices
- 4 grams baking powder
- 240 milliliters milk
- 75 grams dry breadcrumbs
- 160 grams all-purpose flour
- Salt, as required
- 1 egg

Directions:

1. Separate the onion slices into rings.
2. In a shallow dish, mix together the flour, baking powder, and salt.
3. In a second dish, add the milk and egg and beat well.
4. In a third dish, place the breadcrumbs.
5. Coat each onion ring with flour mixture, then dip into egg mixture and finally, coat evenly with the breadcrumbs.
6. Set the temperature of Air Fryer to 185 degrees C and preheat for 5 minutes.
7. After preheating, arrange the onion rings into the air fryer basket in a single layer.
8. Slide the basket in Air Fryer and set the time for 10 minutes.
9. Serve hot.

Tortilla Chips

Servings|3   Time|13 minutes

Nutritional Content (per serving):

Cal| 90   Fat| 3.2g   Protein| 1.8g   Carbs| 14.3g

Ingredients:

- ❖ 4 corn tortillas, cut into triangles
- ❖ Salt, as required
- ❖ 10 milliliters olive oil

Directions:

1. Set the temperature of Air Fryer to 200 degrees C and preheat for 5 minutes.
2. Coat the tortilla chips with oil and sprinkle with salt.
3. After preheating, arrange the tortillas triangles into the greased Air Fryer basket in a single layer.
4. Slide the basket in Air Fryer and set the time for 3 minutes.
5. Transfer the tortilla chips into a large bowl and set aside to cool completely before serving.

Crispy Eggplant Slices

Servings|4   Time|31 minutes

Nutritional Content (per serving):

Cal| 354   Fat| 18.4g   Protein| 9.7g   Carbs| 39.8g

Ingredients:

- ❖ 1 medium eggplant, peeled and cut into ½-inch round slices
- ❖ 2 eggs, beaten
- ❖ 60 milliliters olive oil
- ❖ Salt, as required
- ❖ 60 grams all-purpose flour
- ❖ 120 grams Italian-style breadcrumbs

Directions:

1. In a colander, add the eggplant slices and sprinkle with salt.
2. Set aside for about 45 minutes
3. With paper towels, pat dry the eggplant slices.
4. Add the flour in a shallow dish.
5. Crack the eggs in a second dish and beat well.
6. In a third dish, mix together the oil, and breadcrumbs.
7. Coat each eggplant slice with flour, then dip into beaten eggs and finally, evenly coat with the breadcrumb mixture.
8. Set the temperature of Air Fryer to 200 degrees C and preheat for 5 minutes.
9. After preheating, arrange half of the eggplant slices in an Air Fryer basket in a single layer.
10. Slide the basket in Air Fryer and set the time for 8 minutes.
11. Repeat with the remaining eggplant slices.
12. Serve hot.

Mozzarella Sticks

Servings|4   Time|39 minutes

Nutritional Content (per serving):

Cal| 255   Fat| 9.3g   Protein| 16.4g   Carbs| 26.1g

Ingredients:

- 35 grams white flour
- 45 milliliters non-fat milk
- 455 grams Mozzarella cheese block cut into 7½x1¼-centimeters sticks
- 2 eggs
- 100 grams plain breadcrumbs

Directions:

1. In a shallow dish, place the flour.
2. In a second dish, mix together the eggs, and milk.
3. In a third dish, place the breadcrumbs.
4. Coat the Mozzarella sticks with flour, then dip into egg mixture and finally, coat evenly with the breadcrumbs.
5. Arrange the Mozzarella sticks onto a baking sheet and freeze for about 1-2 hours.
6. Set the temperature of Air Fryer to 225 degrees C and preheat for 5 minutes.
7. After preheating, arrange the Mozzarella sticks into the lightly greased air fryer basket in a single layer in 2 batches.
8. Slide the basket in Air Fryer and set the time for 12 minutes.
9. Serve warm.

Potato Croquettes

Servings|4   Time|38 minutes

Nutritional Content (per serving):

Cal| 297   Fat| 14.2g   Protein| 12.1g   Carbs| 31.3g

Ingredients:

- ❖ 2 medium Russet potatoes, peeled and cubed
- ❖ 1 egg yolk
- ❖ 7 grams fresh chives, minced
- ❖ Pinch of ground nutmeg
- ❖ 2 eggs
- ❖ 60 grams breadcrumbs
- ❖ 15 grams all-purpose flour
- ❖ 55 grams Parmesan cheese, grated
- ❖ 7 grams fresh chives, minced
- ❖ Salt and ground black pepper, as required
- ❖ 30 milliliters vegetable oil

Directions:

1. Add potatoes in the pan of a boiling water and cook for about 15 minutes.
2. Drain the potatoes well and transfer into a large bowl.
3. With a potato masher, mash the potatoes and set aside to cool completely.
4. In the same bowl of mashed potatoes, add in the flour, Parmesan cheese, egg yolk, chives, nutmeg, salt, and black pepper. Whisk until well combined.
5. Make small equal-sized balls from the mixture.
6. Now, roll each ball into a cylinder shape.
7. In a shallow dish, crack the eggs and beat well.
8. In another dish, mix together the breadcrumbs, and oil.
9. Dip the croquettes in egg mixture and then evenly coat with the breadcrumb mixture.
10. Set the temperature of Air Fryer to 200 degrees C and preheat for 5 minutes.
11. After preheating, arrange the croquettes in an Air Fryer basket in a single layer.
12. Slide the basket in Air Fryer and set the time for 7-8 minutes.
13. Serve warm.

Cheese Pastries

Servings|6   Time|20 minutes

Nutritional Content (per serving):

Cal| 135   Fat| 9.8g   Protein| 4.2g   Carbs| 8.1g

Ingredients:

- ❖ 1 egg yolk
- ❖ 1 scallion, finely chopped
- ❖ Salt and ground black pepper, as required
- ❖ 30 milliliters olive oil
- ❖ 115 grams feta cheese, crumbled
- ❖ 3 grams fresh parsley, finely chopped
- ❖ 2 filo pastry sheets (frozen), thawed

Directions:

1. In a glass bowl, add the egg yolk, and with a wire whisk, beat well.
2. Add the feta, parsley, scallion, salt, and black pepper and stir to combine well.
3. Cut each pastry sheet in 3 equal-sized strips.
4. Add a little egg yolk mixture onto the underside of a pastry strip.
5. Fold the tip of pastry sheet over the filling in a zigzag pattern to shape into a triangle.
6. Repeat with the remaining pastry strips and filling.
7. Set the temperature of Air Fryer to 200 degrees C and preheat for 5 minutes.
8. Brush the pastries with oil evenly.
9. After preheating, arrange the pastries into the greased Air Fryer basket in a single layer.
10. Slide the basket in Air Fryer and set the time for 3 minutes.
11. Now set the temperature of Ai Fryer to 185 degrees C for 2 minutes.
12. Serve warm.

Cod Sticks

Servings|2   Time|22 minutes

Nutritional Content (per serving):

Cal| 483   Fat| 10.3g   Protein| 55.3g   Carbs| 38.3g

Ingredients:

- ❖ 3 (115-gram) skinless cod fillets, cut into rectangular pieces
- ❖ 2 garlic cloves, minced
- ❖ Salt and ground black pepper, as required
- ❖ 100 grams flour
- ❖ 4 eggs
- ❖ 1 green chili, finely chopped
- ❖ 10 milliliters light soy sauce

Directions:

1. In a shallow bowl, add the flour.
2. In another bowl, mix well eggs, garlic, green chili, soy sauce, salt, and black pepper.
3. Coat each piece with flour and then, dip into the egg mixture.
4. Set the temperature of Air Fryer to 190 degrees C and preheat for 5 minutes.
5. After preheating, arrange the cod pieces into the greased Air Fryer basket in a single layer.
6. Slide the basket in Air Fryer and set the time for 7 minutes.
7. Serve warm.

Bacon-Wrapped Shrimp

Servings|6   Time|23 minutes

Nutritional Content (per serving):

Cal| 458   Fat| 31.7g   Protein| 40.3g   Carbs| 1.1g

Ingredients:

- ❖ 455 grams shrimp, peeled and deveined
- ❖ 455 grams bacon, thinly slic

Directions:

1. Wrap each shrimp with one bacon slice.
2. Place the shrimp into a baking dish and refrigerate for about 20 minutes.
3. Set the temperature of Air Fryer to 200 degrees C and preheat for 5 minutes.
4. After preheating, arrange the shrimp into the air fryer basket.
5. Slide the basket in Air Fryer and set the time for 7 minutes.
6. Serve warm.

Buffalo Chicken Wings

Servings|4   Time|37 minutes

Nutritional Content (per serving):

Cal| 313   Fat| 13.6g   Protein| 44.6g   Carbs| 0.9g

Ingredients:

- ❖ 910 grams chicken wings, cut into drumettes and flats
- ❖ Ground black pepper, as required
- ❖ 78 grams red hot sauce
- ❖ 5 grams chicken seasoning
- ❖ 5 grams garlic powder
- ❖ 1 5 milliliters olive oil
- ❖ 30 milliliters low-sodium soy sauce

Directions:

1. Sprinkle each chicken wing with chicken seasoning, garlic powder, and black pepper evenly.
2. Set the temperature of Air Fryer to 205 degrees C and preheat for 5 minutes.
3. Arrange the chicken wings into the greased air fryer basket.
4. Slide the basket in Air Fryer and set the time for 10 minutes.
5. Shake the basket once halfway through.
6. Remove from Air Fryer and transfer the chicken wings into a bowl.
7. Drizzle with the red hot sauce, oil, and soy sauce and toss to coat well.
8. Again, arrange the chicken wings into the air fryer basket in a single layer and slide in Air Fryer.
9. Set the temperature of Air Fryer to 205 degrees C for 12 minutes.
10. Serve hot.

Dessert Recipes

Stuffed Apples

Servings|4   Time|28 minutes

Nutritional Content (per serving):

Cal| 378   Fat| 18.4g   Protein| 5.4g   Carbs| 54.7g

Ingredients:

For Stuffed Apples

- ❖ 4 small firm apples, cored
- ❖ 75 grams golden raisins
- ❖ 25 grams sugar

For Vanilla Sauce

- ❖ 120 grams whipped cream
- ❖ 25 grams sugar
- ❖ 2½ milliliters vanilla extract

Directions:

1. In a food processor, add raisins, almonds, and sugar and pulse until chopped.
2. Carefully, stuff each apple with raisin mixture. Line a baking dish with parchment paper.
3. Arrange the apples into the prepared baking dish.
4. Set the temperature of Air Fryer to 180 degrees C and preheat for 5 minutes.
5. After preheating, arrange the baking dish into the air fryer basket.
6. Slide the basket in Air Fryer and set the time for 10 minutes.
7. Meanwhile, for vanilla sauce: in a pan, add the cream, sugar, and vanilla extract over medium heat and cook for about 2-3 minutes or until sugar is dissolved, stirring continuously.
8. Remove the baking dish from Air Fryer and transfer the apples onto plates to cool slightly.
9. Top with the vanilla sauce and serve.

Banana Split

Servings|8   Time|29 minutes

Nutritional Content (per serving):

Cal| 251   Fat| 10.3g   Protein| 4.1g   Carbs| 29.2g

Ingredients:

- 45 milliliters olive oil
- 80 grams corn flour
- 4 bananas, peeled and halved lengthwise
- 30 grams walnuts, chopped
- 120 grams panko breadcrumbs
- 2 eggs
- 40 grams sugar
- 1¼ grams ground cinnamon

Directions:

1. In a medium skillet, heat the oil over medium heat and cook breadcrumbs for about 3-4 minutes or until golden browned and crumbled, stirring continuously.
2. Transfer the breadcrumbs into a shallow bowl and set aside to cool.
3. In a second bowl, place the corn flour.
4. In a third bowl, whisk the eggs.
5. Coat the banana slices with flour, then, dip into eggs and finally, coat evenly with the breadcrumbs.
6. In a small bowl, mix together the sugar and cinnamon
7. Set the temperature of Air Fryer to 140 degrees C and preheat for 5 minutes.
8. After preheating, arrange banana slices into the greased Air Fryer basket in a single layer and sprinkle with cinnamon sugar
9. Slide the basket in Air Fryer and set the time for 10 minutes.
10. transfer the banana slices onto plates and set aside to cool slightly
11. Sprinkle with chopped walnuts and serve.

Shortbread Fingers

Servings|10   Time|27 minutes

Nutritional Content (per serving):

Cal| 224   Fat| 15g   Protein| 2.3g   Carbs| 22.6g

Ingredients:

- ❖ 75 grams caster sugar
- ❖ 170 grams butter
- ❖ 170 grams plain flour

Directions:

1. In a large bowl, mix together the sugar and flour.
2. Add the butter and mix until a smooth dough forms.
3. Cut the dough into 10 equal-sized fingers. With a fork, lightly prick the fingers.
4. Arrange fingers onto the greased baking sheet in a single layer.
5. Set the temperature of Air Fryer to 175 degrees C and preheat for 5 minutes.
6. After preheating, arrange the baking sheet into the air fryer basket.
7. Slide the basket in Air Fryer and set the time for 12 minutes.
8. Remove the baking sheet from Air Fryer and place onto a wire rack to cool for about 5-10 minutes.
9. Now, invert the shortbread fingers onto the wire rack to completely cool before serving.

Chocolate Soufflé

Servings|2   Time|31 minutes

Nutritional Content (per serving):

Cal| 603   Fat| 39.4g   Protein| 9.8g   Carbs| 54g

Ingredients:

- ❖ 85 grams chocolate, chopped
- ❖ 40 grams sugar
- ❖ 5 grams powdered sugar plus extra for dusting
- ❖ 55 grams butter
- ❖ 2 eggs (separated)
- ❖ 2½ milliliters vanilla extract
- ❖ 15 grams all-purpose flour

Directions:

1. In a microwave-safe bowl, put the butter, and chocolate and microwave on high heat for about 2 minutes or until melted completely, stirring after every 30 seconds.
2. Remove from microwave and stir the mixture until smooth.
3. In another bowl, add the egg yolks and beat well.
4. Add the sugar and vanilla extract and beat well.
5. Add the chocolate mixture and mix until well combined.
6. Add the flour and mix well.
7. In a clean glass bowl, add the egg whites and beat until soft peaks form.
8. Fold the whipped egg whites in 3 portions into the chocolate mixture.
9. Grease 2 ramekins and sprinkle each with a pinch of sugar.
10. Place mixture evenly into the prepared ramekins and with the back of a spoon, smooth the top surface.
11. Set the temperature of Air Fryer to 180 degrees C and preheat for 5 minutes.
12. Turn the "Time Knob" to set the time for 14 minutes.
13. After preheating, arrange the ramekins into Air Fryer basket.
14. Slide the basket in Air Fryer and set the time for
15. When the cooking time is completed, open the lid and set the ramekins aside to cool slightly.
16. Sprinkle with the powdered sugar and serve warm.

Brownie Muffins

Servings|12   Time|20 minutes

Nutritional Content (per serving):

Cal| 241   Fat| 9.6g   Protein| 2.8g   Carbs| 36.9g

Ingredients:

- ❖ 1 package Betty Crocker fudge brownie mix
- ❖ 1 egg
- ❖ 10 milliliters water
- ❖ 25 grams walnuts, chopped
- ❖ 90 milliliters vegetable oil

Directions:

1. In a bowl, add all the ingredients and mix well.
2. Place mixture into 12 greased muffin molds.
3. Set the temperature of Air Fryer to 150 degrees C and preheat for 5 minutes.
4. After preheating, arrange the muffin molds into the air fryer basket.
5. Slide the basket in Air Fryer and set the time for 10 minutes.
6. Remove the muffin molds from Air Fryer and place onto a wire rack to cool for about 10 minutes.
7. Carefully invert the muffins onto wire rack to completely cool before serving.

Raspberry Cupcakes

Servings|10   Time|30 minutes

Nutritional Content (per serving):

Cal| 209   Fat| 12.5g   Protein| 2.7g   Carbs| 22.6g

Ingredients:

- ❖ 125 grams self-rising flour
- ❖ Pinch of salt
- ❖ 135 grams butter, softened
- ❖ 2 eggs
- ❖ 65 grams fresh raspberries
- ❖ 2 grams baking powder
- ❖ 15 grams cream cheese, softened
- ❖ 120 grams caster sugar
- ❖ 10 milliliters fresh lemon juice

Directions:

1. In a bowl, mix together flour, baking powder, and salt.
2. In another bowl, mix together the cream cheese, and butter.
3. Add the sugar and whisk until fluffy and light.
4. Now, place the eggs, one at a time and whisk until just combined.
5. Add the flour mixture and stir until well combined.
6. Stir in the lemon juice.
7. Place the mixture into silicon cups and top each with 2 raspberries.
8. Set the temperature of Air Fryer to 185 degrees C and preheat for 5 minutes.
9. After preheating, arrange the silicon cups into an Air Fryer basket.
10. Slide the basket in Air Fryer and set the time for 15 minutes.
11. Remove the silicon cups from Air Fryer and place onto a wire rack to cool for about 10 minutes.
12. Now, invert the cupcakes onto wire rack to completely cool before serving.

Lava Cake

Servings|4   Time|22½ minutes

Nutritional Content (per serving):

Cal| 516   Fat| 32.2g   Protein| 5.2g   Carbs| 51.7g

Ingredients:

- ❖ 115 grams chocolate chips
- ❖ 2 large eggs
- ❖ 130 grams confectioners' sugar
- ❖ 11¼ grams all-purpose flour
- ❖ 47 grams fresh raspberries
- ❖ 113 grams unsalted butter, softened
- ❖ 2 large egg yolks
- ❖ 5 milliliters peppermint extract
- ❖ 15 grams powdered sugar

Directions:

1. In a microwave-safe bowl, add chocolate chips and butter and microwave on high heat for about 30 seconds.
2. Remove the bowl of butter mixture from microwave and stir well.
3. Add the eggs, egg yolks and confectioners' sugar and with a wire whisk, whisk until well combined.
4. Add the flour and gently stir.
5. Lightly grease 4 ramekins and then dust each with a little flour.
6. Place the chocolate mixture into the prepared ramekins evenly.
7. Set the temperature of Air Fryer to 190 degrees C and preheat for 5 minutes.
8. After preheating, arrange the ramekins into the air fryer basket.
9. Slide the basket in Air Fryer and set the time for 12 minutes.
10. Place the ramekins of cakes onto a wire rack for about 4-5 minutes.
11. Carefully run a knife around the edges of a ramekin several times to loosen the cake.
12. Repeat with the remaining ramekins.
13. Dust with powdered sugar and serve immediately with the garnishing of raspberries.

Chocolate Cake

Servings|6   Time|40 minutes

Nutritional Content (per serving):

Cal| 393   Fat| 23.1g   Protein| 7.2g   Carbs| 43.8g

Ingredients:

- 130 grams flour
- 4 grams baking powder
- Pinch of salt
- 130 grams sugar
- 115 grams butter, softened
- 45 grams cocoa powder
- 2 grams baking soda
- 3 eggs
- 120 grams sour cream
- 10 milliliters vanilla extract

Directions:

1. In a large bowl, mix well flour, cocoa powder, baking powder, baking soda, and salt.
2. Add the remaining Ingredients: and with an electric whisker, whisk on low speed until well combined.
3. Set the temperature of Air Fryer to 160 degrees C and preheat for 5 minutes.
4. Place mixture into a greased cake pan.
5. After preheating, arrange the cake pan into an Air Fryer basket.
6. Slide the basket in Air Fryer and set the time for 25 minutes.
7. Remove the cake pan from Air Fryer and place onto a wire rack to cool for about 10 minutes.
8. Now, invert the cake onto wire rack to completely cool before slicing.
9. Cut the cake into desired sized slices and serve.

Cherry Clafoutis

Servings|4   Time|40 minutes

Nutritional Content (per serving):

Cal| 309   Fat| 10.4g   Protein| 3.5g   Carbs| 45g

Ingredients:

- ❖ 332 grams fresh cherries, pitted
- ❖ 32½ grams flour
- ❖ Pinch of salt
- ❖ 1 egg
- ❖ 33 grams powdered sugar
- ❖ 45 milliliters vodka
- ❖ 25 grams sugar
- ❖ 120 grams sour cream
- ❖ 15 grams butter

Directions:

1. In a bowl, mix together the cherries and vodka.
2. In another bowl, add the flour, sugar, and salt and mix well.
3. Add the sour cream, and egg and mix until a smooth dough forms.
4. Place flour mixture evenly into a greased cake pan.
5. Spread cherry mixture over the dough.
6. Place butter on top in the form of dots.
7. Set the temperature of Air Fryer to 180 degrees C and preheat for 5 minutes.
8. After preheating, arrange the cake pan into the air fryer basket.
9. Slide the basket in Air Fryer and set the time for 25 minutes.
10. Remove the cake pan from air fryer and place onto a wire rack to cool for about 10 minutes.
11. Now, invert the Clafoutis onto a platter and sprinkle with powdered sugar.
12. Cut the Clafoutis into desired size slices and serve warm.

Fruity Tacos

Servings|2   Time|15 minutes

Nutritional Content (per serving):

Cal| 212   Fat| 0.9g   Protein| 1.8g   Carbs| 51.6g

Ingredients:

- ❖ 2 soft shell tortillas
- ❖ 50 grams fresh blueberries
- ❖ 25 grams powdered sugar
- ❖ 70 grams strawberry jelly
- ❖ 35 grams fresh raspberries

Directions:

1. Arrange the tortillas onto a smooth surface.
2. Spread about 30-35 grams of strawberry jelly over each tortilla and top each with berries.
3. Sprinkle each with the powdered sugar.
4. Set the temperature of Air Fryer to 150 degrees C and preheat for 5 minutes.
5. After preheating, arrange tortillas into the greased Air Fryer basket.
6. Slide the basket in Air Fryer and set the time for 5 minutes or until crispy.
7. Serve warm.

Apple Pie

Servings|6   Time|45 minutes

Nutritional Content (per serving):

Cal| 190   Fat| 3.1g   Protein| 11.3g   Carbs| 25.3g

Ingredients:

- ❖ 1 frozen pie crust, thawed
- ❖ 40 grams sugar, divided
- ❖ 10 grams ground cinnamon
- ❖ 2½ milliliters vanilla extract
- ❖ 1 egg, beaten

- ❖ 1 large apple, peeled, cored and chopped
- ❖ 10 milliliters fresh lemon juice
- ❖ 15 grams butter, chopped

Directions:

1. With a smaller baking tin, cut 1 crust from thawed pie crust about 1/8-inch larger than pie pan.
2. Now, cut the second crust from the pie crust a little smaller than first one.
3. Arrange the large crust in the bottom of a greased pie pan.
4. In a bowl, mix together the apple, 25 grams of sugar, cinnamon, lemon juice, and vanilla extract.
5. Place apple mixture evenly over the bottom crust.
6. Add the chopped butter over apple mixture.
7. Arrange the second crust on top and pinch the edges to seal.
8. Carefully, cut 3-4 slits in the top crust.
9. Spread the beaten egg evenly over top crust and sprinkle with the remaining sugar.
10. Set the temperature of Air Fryer to 160 degrees C and preheat for 5 minutes.
11. After preheating, arrange the pie pan into an Air Fryer basket.
12. Slide the basket in Air Fryer and set the time for 30 minutes.
13. Place the pie pan onto a wire rack to cool for about 10-15 minutes before serving.
14. Serve warm.

Doughnuts Pudding

Servings|4   Time|1¼ hours

Nutritional Content (per serving):

Cal| 491   Fat| 33.5g   Protein| 5.3g   Carbs| 46,3g

Ingredients:

- ❖ 6 glazed doughnuts, cut into bite-sized pieces
- ❖ 80 grams semi-sweet chocolate chips
- ❖ 4 egg yolks
- ❖ 170 grams sweet cherries (frozen)
- ❖ 75 grams raisins
- ❖ 50 grams sugar
- ❖ 5 grams ground cinnamon
- ❖ 360 grams whipped cream

Directions:

1. In a mixing bowl, combine the doughnut pieces, raisins, cherries, chocolate chips, sugar, and cinnamon.
2. In a second bowl, add egg yolks, and whipping cream and with a beater, whisk until well blended.
3. In the bowl of doughnut mixture, add the egg yolk mixture and mix well.
4. Set the temperature of Air Fryer to 155 degrees C and preheat for 5 minutes.
5. Place doughnuts mixture into a foil-lined baking dish evenly.
6. After preheating, arrange the baking dish into an Air Fryer basket.
7. Slide the basket in Air Fryer and set the time for 60 minutes.
8. Serve warm.

Fudge Brownies

Servings|8   Time|35 minutes

Nutritional Content (per serving):

Cal| 255   Fat| 13.4g   Protein| 3.8g   Carbs| 24.8g

Ingredients:

- ❖ 200 grams sugar
- ❖ 65 grams flour
- ❖ 4 grams baking powder
- ❖ 5 milliliters vanilla extract
- ❖ 113 grams butter, melted
- ❖ 45 grams cocoa powder
- ❖ 2 eggs

Directions:

1. In a large bowl, add the sugar, and butter and whisk until light and fluffy.
2. Add the remaining ingredients and mix until well combined.
3. Place mixture into a greased baking pan and with the back of a spatula, smooth the top surface.
4. Set the temperature of Air Fryer to 175 degrees C and preheat for 5 minutes.
5. After preheating, arrange the baking pan into the air fryer basket.
6. Slide the basket in Air Fryer and set the time for 20 minutes.
7. Remove the baking pan from air fryer and set aside to cool completely.
8. Cut into 8 equal-sized squares and serve.

Thank you for going through the book, I sincerely hope you enjoyed the recipes.

As I said before, a lot of time went into creating so many recipes and I really hope you're satisfied with the recipes provided.

I'm trying really hard to create the best recipes I can and I'm always open to feedback so whether you liked or disliked the book feel free to write on my email at deliciousrecipes.publishing@gmail.com. I always reply and love to communicate with everybody. If you didn't like the recipes you can reach out and I'll share another cookbook or two for free in order to try to improve your experience at least a little bit.

Thank you for going through the recipes, enjoy!

Index

A

apple, 30, 114, 124
applesauce, 30
asparagus, 71
avocado oil, 52

B

bacon, 21, 22, 24, 45, 52, 111
baking powder, 28, 29, 30, 31, 32, 104, 119, 121, 126
baking soda, 31, 32, 121
balsamic vinegar, 87, 91
banana, 29, 115
basil, 44, 45, 79, 82
BBQ sauce, 59
beef round roast, 51
black pepper, 21, 22, 23, 25, 26, 35, 36, 37, 38, 39, 40, 42, 43, 45, 46, 48, 49, 51, 52, 53, 54, 55, 58, 59, 61, 62, 63, 64, 66, 68, 69, 71, 77, 80, 81, 82, 84, 85, 86, 87, 88, 91, 95, 96, 100, 103, 108, 109, 110, 112
blueberries, 123
bread slices, 19, 20, 21, 22
breadcrumbs, 44, 49, 54, 58, 72, 74, 87, 104, 106, 107, 108, 115
Brussels sprouts, 62, 87
butter, 25, 28, 29, 53, 79, 81, 84, 85, 89, 90, 100, 116, 117, 119, 120, 121, 122, 124, 126
buttermilk, 39

C

Cajun seasoning, 76
capsicum, 27, 95
carrots, 89, 98
cashews, 100
catfish, 76
cayenne pepper, 37, 51, 63, 69, 78, 91, 103
cheddar cheese, 23
cherries, 122, 125
chicken breasts, 43, 44, 45
chicken drumsticks, 40, 41
chicken legs, 38, 39
chicken seasoning, 112
chicken thighs, 42
chicken wings, 112

Chile lime seasoning, 97
chives, 79, 84, 108
chocolate, 117, 120, 125
chocolate chips, 120, 125
cilantro, 49, 80
cinnamon, 30, 31, 32, 63, 115, 124, 125
cocoa powder, 121, 126
cod, 72, 110
Colby Jack cheese, 27
cooking spray, 55, 72, 82, 97
cornflakes, 73
Cornish game hen, 35
cornmeal polenta, 76
cream, 23, 25, 33, 82, 84, 114, 119, 121, 122, 125
cream cheese, 119
cumin, 19, 38, 39, 49, 63, 66, 80, 88, 95

D

dill, 71, 72
doughnuts, 125

E

egg, 20, 21, 22, 23, 25, 28, 33, 44, 49, 58, 73, 74, 77, 98, 104, 107, 108, 109, 110, 117, 118, 120, 122, 124, 125
eggplant, 106

F

fennel seed, 27
feta cheese, 26, 85, 109
filet mignon, 52
filo pastry sheets, 109
fish sauce, 45
five-spice powder, 92
flounder, 74
flour, 19, 25, 28, 29, 30, 31, 32, 33, 39, 54, 58, 72, 104, 106, 107, 108, 110, 115, 116, 117, 119, 120, 121, 122, 126
French fried onions, 93
fresh ginger, 38, 41, 63, 75
fudge brownie mix, 118

ricotta cheese, 21
rosemary, 35, 40, 47, 48, 61, 62, 66, 103

S

sage, 47, 93
salmon, 25, 68, 69, 70, 71
salsa verde, 49
salt, 23, 25, 26, 27, 30, 31, 32, 33, 36, 38, 40, 43, 45,
46, 48, 52, 53, 57, 58, 59, 61, 62, 64, 68, 70, 71, 72,
76, 77, 81, 82, 85, 86, 87, 91, 98, 101, 104, 105, 106,
108, 109, 110, 119, 121, 122
sausage, 27
scallion, 25, 109
scallops, 81, 82
sesame seeds, 77, 98
shrimp, 78, 79, 80, 111
sirloin steaks, 54, 63
soy sauce, 56, 75, 92, 94, 98, 110, 112
spinach, 26, 82, 85, 97
Sriracha, 57, 98
sugar, 20, 28, 29, 30, 31, 32, 33, 35, 45, 47, 56, 75, 89,
103, 114, 115, 116, 117, 119, 120, 121, 122, 123,
124, 125, 126

T

thyme, 35, 37, 40, 47, 61, 62, 66, 81
tilapia, 73
tomato, 26, 82, 94
tomato paste, 82

tortillas, 105, 123
tuna, 77
turkey breast, 46, 47
turkey legs, 48
turmeric, 19, 41, 96

V

vanilla extract, 20, 28, 29, 31, 114, 117, 121, 124, 126
vegetable oil, 31, 44, 58, 73, 74, 88, 98, 108, 118
vodka, 122

W

walnuts, 29, 31, 115, 118
water, 25, 45, 98, 102, 108, 118
whiskey, 60
white pepper, 37, 98
whole chicken, 36, 37
wine, 75, 79, 90
Worcestershire sauce, 53, 55

Y

yeast, 33, 96
yogurt, 38, 95

Z

zucchini, 31

Printed in Great Britain
by Amazon